Introduction to the Whole Food Plant Based Lifestyle to Restore Your Health

How 5 Healthy Habits Can Transform Your Life, Regain Your Mind & Body and Reward You with Youthful Longevity

By

Stefan Rieder

By reading this document, the reader agrees that under no circumstances is the author responsible for any losses, direct or indirect, which are incurred as a result of the use of the information contained within this document, including, but not limited to, — errors, omissions, or inaccuracies.

Medical Disclaimer: This info is based on my own experiences and knowledge over the past years. The Content is not intended to substitute for professional medical advice, diagnosis, or treatment. Always seek the advice of your physician or another qualified health provider with any questions you may have regarding a medical condition. Never disregard professional medical advice or delay seeking it because of something you have read in this book.

Table of Contents

Just For You!

A Free Gift to Our Readers

Whole Food Plant-Based Lifestyle Guide to Restore Your Health

Scan the QR code below to download:

http://bit.ly/WFPBLGuide

Introduction

"An estimated 17.9 million people died from cardiovascular diseases in the world in 2019, representing 32% of all global deaths. Of these deaths, 85% were due to heart attack or stroke."

– World Health Organization (WHO).

Do these statistics startle you? They surprised me too! Cardiovascular diseases have been one of the most common causes of deaths across the globe. These diseases are a group of heart and blood vessel disorders and can leave your body weak and damaged forever. Often, these diseases come without any symptoms, so detecting them without a regular check-up becomes difficult.

When my father passed away at the age of 61 from a massive heart attack, his autopsy showed blockages of his arteries with plaque that decreased blood flow to his heart and body. It should have served as a wake-up call for me, considering how similar our lifestyles were! But I continued to live my life in the same way until I was 49 years old and experienced a near-death heart ailment.

While I was on my way to recovery, I was determined never to go down the same path and to become fit and healthy again. I wanted to regain my strength and stamina. That's when I decided to transition to a whole food, plant-based (WFPB) lifestyle. I focused on eating fruits and vegetables and on cutting down on refined and animal-based products, including dairy.

I have seen that people who are at risk or have battled any cardiovascular disease in the past are always on medication. If you are on medications, I'm not recommending you stop taking them unless you first consult with your doctor. Many of these pharmaceuticals lead to a sedentary lifestyle filled with limitations. As a result, these people are more likely to give up on their favorite activities, whether sports, walking, or hiking through the wilderness. In addition to the physical limitations, such a lifestyle also leads to increased anxiety levels, lack of motivation, and even prolonged sadness.

The ill effects of these diseases and their treatment made me ponder over their impact on our daily lives. Perhaps you have thought about this too; you might ask, "How do I prevent myself and my loved ones from getting these diseases," or "How do I, at least, reduce the risk of dying young?" The short answer lies in closely looking at our eating and other lifestyle habits and making healthier choices.

The notion that diet is essential for preventing and treating diseases was first widely accepted because Hippocrates – the father of modern medicine – preached it. He worked extensively to replace superstitions around medication and diet with data-based experiments.

He was famously quoted as saying:

"Let food be thy medicine and medicine be thy food."

Our understanding of food has come a long way since then, but the essence of Hippocrates' advice remains relevant to us.

Did you know that an average American eats junk food, laden with preservatives, once every four days? When combined with low levels of daily physical activity, this means the risk of cardiovascular diseases is very high. If steaks and burgers are your staple diet, it is time for you to take your health more seriously.

The human body is designed to survive, and survival depends on the food we eat. Therefore, it is crucial to give our bodies an optimum ratio of micronutrients and macronutrients to carry out daily bodily functions effectively. Modern medicine can help us in alleviating the symptoms of illnesses. However, there are natural ways to guard our bodies against diseases so that we never have to feel the ill effects of the disease. One of the best natural methods of keeping our body strong and immune to diseases is maintaining a healthy diet.

I consulted many nutritionists, read multiple books and research papers, and even experimented with many types of diets myself. While most diets made my gut feel good, I experienced improved energy levels and elimination of my body-aches with the plant-based (WFPB) diet. When followed correctly, this diet can help improve your quality of life – just like it improved mine!

Before I address the different aspects of a WFPB diet, it might help to consider what "WFPB" actually means.

A whole food, plant-based diet is centered on whole, unrefined, or minimally refined plants. It's a diet based on fruits, vegetables, tubers, whole grains, and legumes; and it excludes meat (including chicken and fish), dairy products, and eggs, as well as highly refined foods like bleached flour, refined sugar, and oil (Forks Over Knives, 2015, para. 1).

The whole food plant-based diet, as its name denotes, requires the exclusion of animal products like meat or dairy. However, if this is your first exposure to this lifestyle, a gradual elimination of meat and dairy over time means you're more likely to stick to the diet.

While people follow this diet to cut down on their consumption of animal products, they do so to varying degrees. But the key is that they make a conscious effort of cutting down and eventually eliminating meat intake, while eating food products that come directly from plants. That's the secret mantra to their good health!

While the convenience of fast foods is appealing, you can't ignore the proven rich health benefits of eating fruits and vegetables. Many of these WFPB foods have multiple hidden healing powers. For example, **kale** is an excellent source of protein. But did you know that it can also help with depression? The omega-3 acids, iron, vitamin B6, and folates help release dopamine and serotonin and thus improve one's mood. Similarly, if your goal is weight loss, **cucumbers** will help you by adding antioxidants to your diet. No matter what your goal is, a WFPB diet will help you in achieving it healthily.

When WFPB food items come with such incredible and miraculous benefits, why should we not fully embrace their power while appreciating the flavors they add to the diet? With the motivation of helping people to live an active and healthy lifestyle, I have written this book to be your go-to guide for WFPB nutrition. My goal is to introduce a new form of lifestyle to you and educate you about its benefits, nutritional values, and overall impact on your life.

This book begins by highlighting the clear distinctions between vegan, plant-based, and vegetarian diets. Often, I have noticed that people use these terms almost interchangeably, due to a lack of a clear understanding of these diet forms. But in reality, there are stark differences between them, with a few overlapping areas. For instance, a WFPB lifestyle is so much more than just following a WFPB diet. There is a lot more to it, which you can explore in the first chapter.

All of us have our perception of heart-related disorders, but most of us are actually quite ill-informed on this subject. In this book, I have addressed this issue. A part of the book sheds light on heart disease, its symptoms, and how a WFPB lifestyle can help reduce the risks of getting heart disease. Most of this knowledge and advice comes from my personal experience of battling atherosclerosis (coronary artery disease) and winning the fight.

While the information will greatly benefit you, I still strongly advise you to visit your doctor to determine if you have heart-related problems. Don't wait for it to become a bigger health issue as I did, resulting in a couple of near-fatal episodes that rocked my family and friends and jolted me into the reality of my mortality!

Every new lifestyle concept comes with its share of myths and concerns. While the WFPB lifestyle has been around for quite some time now, some myths around the subject still need to be debunked. This book will address the elephant in the room by debunking the myths related to a WFPB diet and the WFPB lifestyle. Not only that, but I have also carefully listed the pros and cons of the diet and lifestyle to enable you to make an informed decision about adopting it.

When we talk about diet, the first question that comes to our mind is, "What can I eat? Will I feel hungry during the day?" I have dedicated a chapter in this book solely to address this question. It will act as a step-by-step guide on what you can consume, the food items you should avoid, and how to graduate to higher levels while following this diet. I will also share the minute changes in your routine that will complement your diet and give you the best results. It is important to remember that every step taken in the right direction matters.

Stress has become an inevitable evil in our lives that can quickly put our health at risk. In today's fast-paced world, it is crucial to manage stress and keep it at bay. But the first step towards managing stress is recognizing it. I have seen many people, including my friends and family, who never realized that they were under continuous stress and needed to break free from it. If you have also felt that, this book can help. The WFPB lifestyle will not only aid in your physical fitness but also assist in an overall improvement in your mental health and stress handling capabilities.

The book sheds light on the recognition and management of all kinds of stress. It will also help you understand the role of a WFPB lifestyle in keeping stress away, along with some basic meditation practices that can help lift your mood and fight the stress.

One of the biggest myths that I have come across is that a WFPB lifestyle is for middle-aged people. But in reality, this lifestyle is for anyone who wishes to lead the healthiest way of life. It doesn't matter if you are a teenager, a young adult, or a middle-aged individual; a healthy diet always paves the way for a healthy lifestyle. In this book, I have written about the impact of a healthy diet coupled with physical activity and exercise for keeping your heart and body fit.

Breathing is essential for our bodies to function but is one of the most underrated and overlooked bodily processes. I have always been a great advocate of focusing on breathing, and the book is a testimonial of the same. In this book, I have emphasized the importance of breathing, its role in helping the human body deal with stress, and how mindful breathing can aid decision-making. I will also share some breathing exercises that will help in improving your cardiovascular and overall health. These exercises certainly helped me in adopting a healthier lifestyle!

We have often heard people say that their heart is 'heavy' with grief, or they are suffering from a 'broken heart,' or feeling 'lighter.' If you think these are metaphorical terms, you are mistaken. There exists a current relationship between our emotions and our heart. With the strong human need to socialize with others, emotions, especially sadness, can seriously impact one's heart and overall well-being. This book will take you through these spiritual heart diseases and what can be done to overcome them. Love and belonging keep the heart happy and a happy heart is the way to a happier lifestyle!

There is no denying the fact that eating healthy and staying fit adds longevity to your life. The last chapter of the book will take you through facts and anecdotes of people who adopted a WFPB lifestyle and lived longer than the population's average age. I have covered how every minor adjustment or replacement in their diet helped keep cardiovascular risks at bay.

I fought my own battle with coronary artery disease, and on recovering, I decided never to venture down that painful path again. Instead, I chose a healthier approach to my well-being and transitioned to a WFPB lifestyle that eventually became a part of my daily routine. I have followed a WFPB lifestyle as described in this book, and I feel great all the time and can't remember the last time I got sick. Moreover, I have been researching this lifestyle, and its benefits continue to amaze me. I want to share this lifestyle approach with you so that you can live a happy, healthy, and long life.

This book will take you through the basics of this lifestyle, its benefits, and how it will work specifically for you. You'll get cues about how to whip up a delectable WFPB meal as well. Whether you are new to this lifestyle, already familiar with it, or already practice it, this book will definitely serve as an invaluable resource and guide.

Let's go on a journey towards better health together!

Part 1

The Lifestyle

Chapter 1
Whole Food Plant Based (WFPB) Vs. Veganism Vs. Vegetarianism

Ever since I adopted a WFPB lifestyle, I have been enthusiastic about spreading awareness of its benefits to anyone who cares to listen. I strongly emphasize its physical and mental health benefits, impact on the environment, and the ease of meal preparation. However, I have often observed that people confuse a WFPB lifestyle with veganism or vegetarianism, so much so that some people even use these terms interchangeably. So, before I delve into the how's of a WFPB lifestyle, you need to understand what it is and how it differs from the other two lifestyles.

In the simplest terms, the central pillar of a WFPB lifestyle is the diet, as described in Chapter 4. This refers to focusing on filling your plate with items that are not processed and that are sourced from plants. That means including fruits, vegetables, nuts, legumes, seeds, and whole grains in your diet. At the same time, it also means cutting down on animal-sourced products initially, including dairy items like milk or curd, and gradually omitting them entirely from your diet. In this diet, the focus is on meeting the body's nutritional needs with minimally processed foods.

A WFPB lifestyle is not just limited to the consumption of whole foods for your meals. There are four other components of the lifestyle that, when combined, represent the healthiest and optimal way of life to reduce the risk of getting heart disease and restore your health and vitality if you have cardiovascular disease. This holistic lifestyle approach also includes the management of your stress, regular exercise and activity, a daily breathing exercise, and fostering love and belonging. It is a complete shift from a life full of stress, illness, and lethargy to a lifestyle approach that helps you reduce stress, breathe more consciously, increase activity, and love and be loved.

Veganism is a form of lifestyle where the main focus is on excluding animal-based products as much as possible. This philosophy is based around avoiding all forms of exploitation of and cruelty to animals, from daily food consumption to clothing, makeup, and accessories. Followers of vegan lifestyles even prefer not to consume any medicine tested on animals.

While there are fewer differences between a WFPB lifestyle and a vegan lifestyle, the vegetarian philosophy is quite different from the other two. Vegetarians do not eat raw or cooked animals. However, they have no reservations about consuming animal-based products like milk, cheese, and curd. Since vegetarianism is less strict than the other two forms of lifestyle, this diet varies depending on what people include and omit in their meals. Some people follow two different types of diets while being vegetarian. On some days, they omit eggs from their plates, while on others, they become strict with a no-animal-product diet.

Lifestyle choice	WFPB	Vegan	Vegetarian
Meat and Poultry	No	No	No
Dairy products like milk and cheese	No	No	Yes
Seafood	No	No	Reduce
Oils	Avoid	Yes	Yes
Processed or packaged food items	No	Yes	Yes
Fruits and vegetables	Yes	Yes	Yes
Animal-tested products like makeup	Yes	No	Yes
Animal skin clothing	Yes	No	Yes

The differences between the three different types of lifestyles may seem small. Yet, each lifestyle can impact your daily life in different ways. The following table will help you understand how these three forms of lifestyle differ from each other. Match your daily lifestyle choices with the table and find out about the kind of lifestyle you lead right now and the one you wish to follow.

Now that we understand the fundamental differences between the three most popular forms of lifestyle, let us dive deep into the goodness of the WFPB lifestyle and how it can lead to a healthy and happy life.

Make a Choice: WFPB Lifestyle

I have noticed that people are often confused about choosing a healthy lifestyle for themselves. They might know the nitty-gritty of all the different lifestyle choices available for them to adopt, but the variances between all of them sets their minds into a whirlwind of questions.

The confusion is understandable. However, there is one thing to keep in mind before going crazy with doubts and apprehensions. You should always adopt a lifestyle that brings you closer to the fresh and naturally produced forms of food items while minimizing the consumption of processed foods (Fox, 2019). After all, being healthy starts with eating healthy.

The WFPB diet does precisely that!

When we talk about a WFPB diet, we are essentially talking about the overall lifestyle described above. We should look at the lifestyle as not limiting us. On the contrary, it allows some flexibility for consuming or involving animal-based products in our lifestyle.

If you are relatively healthy, that is, you don't have heart disease, the occasional consumption of animal-based food is okay. I occasionally have a piece of birthday cake at a party or enjoy my wife's fabulously good banana bread, and these items have dairy in them. I very rarely, once or twice a year, eat wild-caught fish. Followers of a WFPB lifestyle mostly thrive on WFPB products, but animal-based food items aren't entirely off-limits for them.

This also applies to those of you who have never followed a WFPB diet. The best practice is to gradually consume more fruits and vegetables, legumes, and whole grains, and, at the same time, reduce your intake of animal-based foods.

For those of you who are currently struggling with heart disease, as I had, it is recommended that you eliminate all forms of animal products from your diet, including all dairy and meat. After at least a year of solely consuming a WFPB diet, you may be able to occasionally veer off the diet without detrimental impacts on your health. The best approach would be to test and monitor your heart disease before starting the WFPB diet and continue testing on a quarterly basis. Once you've determined that the diet and lifestyle are working and you're seeing marked improvements to your heart health, then it may be time to eat a cookie or a wild-caught piece of salmon occasionally.

The Pentagon of a Plant-Based Diet

As is clear from the name, a WFPB diet focuses on food items obtained directly from plants. There is a rich array of WFPB food items abundant in vitamins and minerals that can lead to overall healthy nutrition for the body. Let us explore the five categories of WFPB foods.

Fruits

Time and again, research has proven that fruits are one of the most integral components of a balanced diet. Fruits are a rich source of vitamins, minerals, fiber, and even water. Each type of fruit contains varying quantities of these elements and a rich number of antioxidants, polyphenols, and phytochemicals. Antioxidants are found in food and produced in our bodies. They prevent or delay cellular damage and protect us from heart disease, premature aging, cancer, and possibly depression and anxiety (Gavin, 2021). Polyphenols are compounds in plants that act as antioxidants. Meaning they neutralize harmful free radicals that damage cells and increase the risk of disease.

Phytochemicals are found in plants, "phyto" meaning plant. Studies have found that phytochemicals reduce the risk of cardiovascular disease, cancer, Type 2 Diabetes and neurodegenerative diseases such as Alzheimer's and Parkinson's (Webb, 2013).

You may be apprehensive about the sugar content of fruits. It's true, fruits are a rich source of naturally occurring sugars. However, each fruit contains a different amount of sugar. Sometimes, due to this reason, people classify fruits into different categories based on their sugar content and abstain from eating fruits with higher sugar content.

It is understood that the health benefits of fruits far outweigh the sugar content (Villines, 2019). Abstaining from eating fruits would lead to the exclusion of essential micronutrients and antioxidants from your diet. Don't fear fruit; savor it!

Vegetables

Vegetables are a vibrant source of vitamins, minerals, dietary fibers, and antioxidants. The green, leafy vegetables are loaded with nutrition and have very few calories. Stalk vegetables, such as celery and asparagus, are rich sources of minerals and folic acid. Due to their low-calorie content and high nutritious value, vegetables are a necessity in your everyday life.

The nutritional value of vegetables naturally depends on the serving that you consume. For instance, calorie count may range from 6.5 calories in a single celery stalk to about 67 calories in half a cup of peas.

While there is no actual portion size that you must adhere to, experts recommend that adults consume up to 7 servings of fruits and vegetables daily.

The health benefits of consuming vegetables are abundant, making them a perfect meal choice for anyone who wants to lead a healthy lifestyle. If you are one of those people, add vegetables to your diet, starting today!

Legumes

Are you one of those people who say that they hate legumes but include peas very often in their meals? If yes, you have been mistaken all your life, because peas belong to the legume family, and you have been eating them all this time!

Legumes are a very balanced source of vitamins, fiber, healthy calories, and essential micro and macronutrients. Some legumes even have calcium content equivalent to a glass of milk. Additionally, they are laden with essential amino acids, antioxidants, and 'resistance starch,' which help control blood sugar levels.

There are more than 16,000 varieties of beans and legumes. Some of the most popular ones include chickpeas, peanuts, black beans, lentils, and soybeans. The nutritional benefits of legumes depend upon the quantity consumed. For instance, if you consume half a cup of cooked black beans, you take in 114 calories, 7.6 g of protein, 20 g of carbohydrates, and zero fat or cholesterol. So, are you going to let go of all these benefits by not consuming beans and legumes?

Whole Grains

Whole grains have been a part of our platters for thousands of years now. And rightly so! They are extremely rich nutrient sources that keep diabetes, high blood pressure, and obesity at bay.

Whole grains are essentially the seeds of grassy plants known as cereals. However, sources of some non-grass plants are also rich in fiber, such as quinoa and amaranth.

Whole grains are made of three layers, each of which is laden with beneficial components. The first layer is called *bran* and is rich in minerals, antioxidants, and fiber. The second layer is called *endosperm* and is the gold mine of healthy carbohydrates. Finally, the third layer is called the *germ*. This layer is an excellent resource of proteins, vitamins, minerals, and plant compounds. With such a power-packed composition, including whole grains in your diet is a must.

Common whole grains include oatmeal, quinoa, buckwheat, millet, sorghum, and brown rice. Refined grains have the bran and germ removed, which leads to a dip in their nutritional components. Therefore, it is important to include whole grains in your diet to extract the maximum benefits.

Tubers or Root Vegetables

Tubers or root vegetables are called functional foods. Like the other four food items of the pentavalent, tubers also offer numerous desirable health benefits such as proteins, antioxidants, and energy. Additionally, tubers have a rich composition of water and thus help maintain the body's ionic requirements. There are 5 essential electrolytes including magnesium, potassium, sodium, chloride, and calcium. These nutritional elements are minerals that separate into positive and negative ions when dissolved in water.

Root vegetables and tubers have a high starch component, so they serve as quick energy resources. The energy component of a root vegetable is one-third of an equivalent quantity of rice or wheat, and the rest of it is moisture content.

Among the tubers, potatoes, sweet potatoes, and yams contain a very high amount of protein. Along with protein and amino acids, they are also a rich source of micronutrients such as potassium, sulfur, and beta-carotene, all of which are essential for the healthy functioning of the human body. Cutting them out from your diet means letting go of their goodness. Don't commit that sin!

With such a vast variety of food items available for your consumption under the WFPB diet, you can mix and match them to your heart's content. The beauty is that there is no "one size fits all" approach. However, the focus is on cutting down the consumption of processed or refined food items and enjoying more natural forms of food. So, fill your plate with fruits, nuts, vegetables, or any earlier mentioned food items and welcome good health and wellness.

Benefits of a WFPB lifestyle

The WFPB diet is a very healthy approach to eating, with a plethora of benefits extending way beyond weight loss. A rich diet centered around whole plant food items and minimal refined or processed food products is sure to benefit your overall health. A very famous New York-based dietician named Maya Feller (Lawler, 2020) embraced this form of lifestyle: "Whether you are an animal lover, an environmental advocate, or want to live your healthiest life, being WFPB is the one underlying thread that seems to be compelling to so many of us," Maya said

Let us look at the host of benefits associated with a WFPB lifestyle that are backed by scientific research.

Keeps your heart healthy

With the focus on consuming food items sourced directly from plants with the least possible processing, we do our tickers a favor. Plants have essential nutrients that are very good for your heart and are challenging to get from other food items. The minerals, vitamins, fiber, phytochemicals, and antioxidants offered by WFPB food items keep your cells healthy and your heart happy. According to expert doctors, a WFPB diet strengthens your immune system and helps fight against harmful germs and microbes.

Many food items sourced from animals, directly or indirectly, such as meat, come with many saturated fats. Scientifically, saturated fats are known to increase the low-density lipoprotein (LDL) cholesterol levels in the body (American Heart Association, 2020), thus contributing to an increase in plaquing of your arteries and making you prone to cardiac illnesses. On the other hand, WFPB food items are rich in unsaturated fatty acids (or good fats) that help keep cholesterol levels under control and cardiac disorders at bay.

Easy weight management

Many people face weight management issues at one point or the other in their lives. To get fit, they may take up slimming medicines, stricter diets, and strenuous workouts. However, a simple solution is to let go of the extra pounds by following a WFPB lifestyle!

When you switch to a WFPB diet, you cut down on many food items that otherwise lead to weight gain. This is because whole WFPB food items are a rich source of fiber that helps fill you up and eventually cut down on your calorie intake. By including 40 gm of fiber in your daily diet, you can control your hunger pangs and ultimately limit your calorie intake. This is possible quickly with a WFPB diet rich in fruits, nuts, vegetables, and whole grains.

With effective weight control, you can keep the bad cholesterol at bay and lower the risk of problems such as high blood pressure, diabetes or heart diseases.

So, swap your meat-heavy diet with a WFPB platter and shed those extra pounds that you always wanted to lose – just like me! I lost 50 pounds in four months solely by eating a WFPB diet.

Reduces inflammation

The essential nutrients from WFPB food items work to curb inflammation levels in the body. The same antioxidants and vitamins that go around in your body while giving immunity also work towards removing the inflammation levels in the body by neutralizing toxins that enter it.

Inflammation is linked to damage of the cells and tissues of the body, which can lead to diseases like cancer or arthritis in severe cases. WFPB food items work towards removing these triggers and reducing the risk of these diseases.

Helps in preventing type II diabetes

Studies have proven that diet and type II diabetes are interrelated. When you cannot control your weight, the accumulated fatty acid cushions the cells and makes them resistant to insulin.

In the case of type II diabetes, diet can significantly impact well-being. Research conducted in 2016 revealed that eating a diet rich in whole plant foods rich in fiber reduces the risk of developing type II diabetes by nearly 34%. This is so because a WFPB diet is low in saturated fats that increase cholesterol levels in the body. With lower levels of cholesterol, chances of developing type II diabetes reduce greatly.

Decreases the risk of cancer

The risk of cancer has increased for everyone due to many factors, including pollution and the consumption of unhealthy food items. However, a study of 69,000 individuals revealed that a WFPB diet was associated with a significantly lower risk of gastro-intestinal or colorectal cancer (*Tatamango-Bartley, 2013*). A WFPB diet reduces the risk of breast cancer in females by up to 25%. The fiber and phytochemicals present in whole plant foods are big contributors to a lowered risk of cancer.

You might be thinking that meat items such as steak are very high in essential nutrients too. So why are they not recommended foods for consumption? A key reason is increased red and processed meat consumption was associated with cancer risk. Higher beef consumption was associated with some cancers (Lippi et al., 2016). When meat items (especially red meat) are cooked, cancer-creating compounds are produced (Aschwanden & Aschwanden, 2015). Also, the consumption of processed meat increases the risk of colorectal cancer (Santarelli et al., 2008). While the risk decreases with less consumption of red and processed meat, the lowest risk is a no-meat diet.

Keeps your brain strong for longer

While there are hundreds of physiological benefits of following a WFPB lifestyle, there are mental benefits too. A WFPB lifestyle can slow down or reverse the cognitive decline that is usually expected in old age.

According to a review of nine studies published in Frontiers in Ageing Neuroscience, consuming an extra 100 grams of fruits every day could lead to a reduction of 13% in the risk of cognitive decline or dementia (Jiang et al., 2017a). The reason for this is simple: fruits are rich in antioxidants and polyphenols. The abundance of these plant compounds in this form of diet help in slowing down the effects of Alzheimer's disease, cognitive impairment, and dementia in old age. So, start including fruits, vegetables, beans, and nuts in your diet to stay mentally fit and healthy even in your old age. A healthy mind paves the way for a healthy life!

Keeps the planet healthy

Adopting a WFPB lifestyle is good for your health and protects the planet by reducing the carbon footprint. When you adopt this lifestyle, sustainable consumption becomes a part of your routine. This helps reduce greenhouse gases, water consumption, usage of land for factory plantations, etc., all of which are among the most significant contributors to global warming.

Statistically, shifting to sustainable WFPB dietary patterns can bring about nearly a 70% reduction in emission of greenhouse gases and a 50% reduction in water usage. Furthermore, increasing your consumption of WFPB food items leads to a boost in the local economy dependent on farming and reduced reliance on unhealthy food production practices in the guise of factory farming. Keeping our planet healthy starts with you, and a WFPB lifestyle will help you get there!

Switching to this kind of routine is not difficult. You can start with making small changes in your diet, such as cutting down on meat and dairy items, including more whole grains on your plate, or increasing your fruit consumption. As you go along, you will notice you're feeling well, less sluggish, and that you're losing weight. You will get accustomed to this lifestyle, and the health benefits that it will bring will amaze you. So, get ready to welcome a happy heart and healthy life! With so many benefits of a WFPB lifestyle, it is worth giving it a try.

Chapter 2
Heart Disease? You Don't Want This!

Until I was in my 40s, I didn't think about having a healthy lifestyle. I was, and still am, very involved in sports and physical activity, and I felt good most of the time, so I ate whatever I wanted to. I was an omnivore and loved steak and burgers, particularly barbequed. All of this continued until the age of 49, when I was diagnosed with severe atherosclerosis, a form of coronary artery disease. On examination, the doctor made it clear that one of my arteries was 100% blocked, and two others were 90% blocked by plaque. Doctors had to perform an emergency triple bypass surgery to better my condition and bring me back to life.

Heart diseases are the number one cause of death in our Western culture.

But why is this so important? I have written this to show you how easily we have become prone to severe cardiac diseases simply because we do not think about or care enough about our health. One of the biggest reasons behind such staggering statistics is the lack of commitment and dedication to a healthy lifestyle. We need to realize that following a healthy lifestyle is not just our best defense against heart problems; it is also a responsibility.

Prevention of heart diseases starts with very small lifestyle changes that have the potential of creating a big impact on our health. Before we learn more about the lifestyle changes we can make to keep our hearts happy and healthy, let us first understand the science behind cardiac diseases.

All about heart diseases

Our heart is a small, fist-sized organ that pumps blood through the network of arteries and veins throughout the body. While it is a very tiny organ, it is extraordinary because of its functions. Our heart is responsible for performing the following four prominent roles in our body:

It pumps clean and oxygenated blood to all parts of the body via arteries.
It receives all the deoxygenated blood containing metabolic waste from all parts of the body via veins.
It pumps the essential hormones and other vital components to different designated organs.
It helps in maintaining optimum blood pressure.

The kind of lifestyle choices we make impact these functions. Poor lifestyles can lead to many heart diseases, some of which are often only detected at later stages and become practically incurable.

Most people think that all heart diseases are similar. However, this is one of the biggest myths that needs debunking. Heart diseases arise from different root causes and can have different impacts on the health of your heart. Due to the differing effects, their treatments also differ from one another.

Types of heart diseases

Regardless of its severity, every heart disease impacts the structural or functional ability of the heart. Conditions with the same root cause can be grouped and follow somewhat similar treatment. Let us understand a few significant types of cardiac diseases:

Coronary artery and vascular disease

This is the same disease I was diagnosed with in 2012. It is one of the most common heart diseases in which the coronary arteries – vessels that supply blood to your heart – are hardened and accumulate plaque that blocks blood flow. This blockage in the arteries leads to a decrease in blood flow to your heart, thereby restricting oxygen flow to it.

Coronary artery disease can lead to severe pain in the chest – a condition called angina – and eventually it can lead to a heart attack or stroke. The risk of such a condition increases greatly if you are inactive, consume food items that aggravate the cholesterol levels in your body, or are obese. So, take a closer look at your diet, include healthier meals like WFPB food items, and keep the risk of coronary artery disease low.

Common symptoms of coronary artery disease include shortness of breath, pain or numbness in the limbs, chest pain or tightness, and pain in the jaw cavity. Consult your doctor as soon as you experience any of these symptoms; early detection is critical.

Heart Rhythm Disorders

A healthy heart beats 60-100 times per minute. Every time our heart beats, electrical impulses are generated that coordinate these beats for the proper functioning of our heart.

Heart rhythm problems or arrhythmias are conditions in which the electrical impulses that coordinate our heartbeats do not work appropriately. This impairment in impulses leads to an improper or irregular beating of the heart. In addition, it further interferes with all the other functions that the heart performs.

There are some specific conditions in which a heightened or lower heartbeat is perfectly normal. For instance, when you exercise, your heart beats faster than usual, because it must quickly supply oxygen to all the body parts. Similarly, during sleep, our heartbeats are relatively slower because of the non-activity of the body. However, if there is an unusually fast or slow beating of the heart when awake but not exercising, it could lead to fainting and sometimes even sudden death.

Common symptoms of heart arrhythmia include fluttering in the chest cavity, racing or slowing heartbeat, fainting, dizziness, or chest pain. Even the mild experience of any of these signs calls for an immediate appointment with your doctor.

Structural heart diseases

Sometimes, heart problems arise due to a deformity in the tissues or valves of the heart. Some structural deformities are present at the time of birth and are called congenital structural diseases. However, there are other kinds of deformities that may develop during your lifetime.

The most common conditions that arise due to structural heart disease include high blood pressure or hypertension. A poorly controlled blood pressure makes the heart work harder than usual to pump blood to all parts of the body. If this continues for an extended time, the extra work may lead to heart failure in severe cases.

Another common condition is a heart valve problem. The primary function of heart valves is to control the direction of blood flow in and out of the heart. They act as doors that regulate the entry and exit of blood. When the valves get damaged, their ability to open and close becomes impaired, which in turn limits the blood flow and hampers its functionality.

While many congenital heart diseases are detected as soon as you are born, others develop during your life and often exhibit symptoms. Common signs of structural heart disease include paleness of skin color, swelling, or inflammation in the lower limbs. In newborns or infants, the earliest symptoms consist of shortness of breath during feeding and a lowered body weight.

Heart failure

As is evident from the name, the heart fails to perform its usual activities and stops working in this condition. Such a situation arises when the heart has been overworked for an extended period.

Heart failure usually happens due to a heart attack or hypertension. However, it can also occur because of severe thyroid disease or an ill-treated heart muscle disease. Common symptoms include breathlessness during day-to-day activities, fatigue, or dizziness.

Signs of a heart attack

According to Centers for Disease Control and Prevention (CDC), about 805,000 people in the US suffer from heart attacks every year (Centers for Disease Control and Prevention, 2021). With this situation becoming more and more common every day, you need to take care of your heart and understand the warning signs of this disease if they persist.

Some of the most common signs and symptoms of a heart attack include the following:

Chest discomfort

This is one of the most common symptoms of a heart attack. It can feel like a squeezing in the chest cavity, pain, or fullness. Chest discomfort usually lasts longer than a few minutes. In some cases, it even goes away and returns. If you feel even a slight pain in your chest, do not hesitate to get medical attention.

Shortness of breath

Many people had reported shortness of breath before they experienced a heart attack. It may or may not be followed by a pain in the chest cavity. It is advisable not to take shortness of breath lightly if it occurs during your day. Reach out to emergency services right away!

Discomfort in the upper cavity of the body

Sometimes, a heart attack is preceded by sudden pain in one or both arms, the neck, jaw, or even stomach. This pain may or may not be followed by a pain in the chest cavity.

Other symptoms

While the other three symptoms are the most common ones experienced during a heart attack, sometimes it is preceded by breaking out in a cold sweat or feeling lightheaded or nauseous.

While most symptoms are common for men and women, some signs are usually found in women. Just like men, women are also highly likely to experience angina or chest pain. However, they are also more likely to experience nausea, vomiting, jaw pain, or shortness of breath than men. Either way, it is advised to reach out to your doctor as soon as you experience these symptoms or any other unusual sign.

Common causes of heart diseases

There can be a myriad of reasons behind the development of heart ailments. While some are directly related to the cardiac health and structure of the entire cardiovascular system, many others are influenced by the lifestyle choices that you make.

Some of the direct causes of heart diseases include the following:
A congenital structural deformity to a part or whole of the heart muscle
Damage to a part of the entire heart
Problems with the entry or exit of blood from the heart chambers
Low oxygen and nutrient supply to the heart
Genetic causes of heart impairment or damage

Along with these reasons, there can be a host of other lifestyle causes of poor heart health. These include:

Obesity
Alcohol and tobacco
Dietary choices (high consumption of meat and dairy)
Increase in low-density lipoproteins (LDL)
Sleep apnea
High blood pressure
Age
Low activity levels (no physical exercise)

Lifestyle changes for a healthy heart

You can assure a healthy heart by making simple lifestyle changes that are easy to adopt. Here are some small lifestyle changes that you can make in your everyday life that will reap tremendous benefits to your heart and your overall health and well-being:

Stop smoking: Tough as it may sound, it is essential. I know it is challenging. But it surely isn't more demanding than recovering from a stroke or a heart attack that will most likely leave your heart weak for the rest of your life.

It won't happen in a single day. But a little progress made every day could help you get to the 'no smoking' zone faster than you would expect.

Physical activity: Daily fitness should be included in your routine. Move your body. It has been demonstrated that dedicating 150 minutes every week towards moderate to high-intensity physical activity can keep your cholesterol and blood sugar levels under control. What's more, it can keep your weight under check, and you will be able to maintain that healthy body that you've always wanted.

Eat healthier meals: When you follow a WFPB diet, more nutritious meals become a part of your routine. It will help you fight all the cardiovascular diseases and make your body strong and healthy.

With a clean diet and coordinated physical activity, you can regulate the consumption and burning of calories just the way you want.

Heart Diseases and Erectile Dysfunction in Men

Erectile Dysfunction (ED) refers to the inability to keep a penile erection firm enough for intercourse. It is estimated that 50% of men will experience some form of erectile dysfunction. For many years, this situation was considered to be related to the psychological health of a man. Stress, depression, and anxiety were believed to be the reasons behind ED.

However, the latest research suggests that underlying vascular or blood flow-related issues are the most common causes of erectile dysfunction. If you are experiencing heart-related issues, especially coronary artery disease, getting the proper treatment for it will also help with the problem of erectile dysfunction.

The early studies of the connection between heart disease and erectile dysfunction suggested that the blockages in the arteries by the accumulation of plaque resulted in restricted blood flow in the penis that leads to difficulty in penile erection. However, recent studies reveal that when erectile dysfunction precedes a heart problem, it is usually due to a dysfunction in the inner lining or endothelium of the blood vessels. The blood supply to the heart and penis is hampered because of atherosclerosis.

Note that erectile dysfunction doesn't always have an underlying heart issue associated with it. It may not be indicative of a heart problem. Nonetheless, whenever erectile dysfunction is detected, it is advisable to get screened for your cardiac health as well.

Psychological causes of erectile dysfunction

While it is already established that erectile dysfunction is often associated with a heart ailment, the psychological reasons behind the condition can't be ignored. The three main psychological issues are related to erectile dysfunction are:

Fear of intimacy: This is touted to be a significant reason behind erectile dysfunction. It is usually associated with relationship problems because of stress or concerns around lack of communication.

Depression: Depression can be a significant reason behind erectile dysfunction. It can decrease the urge for intercourse and thus cause problems with penile erections.

General anxiety: Mental health issues such as anxiety can cause impairment between brain signals and physical bodily responses. This can lead to decreased blood flow in the penis, leading to erection problems during intercourse.

Common risk factors between erectile dysfunction and heart diseases

Erectile Dysfunction and heart diseases have one thing in common – both happen due to an obstruction in the flow of blood. The commonality also exists in the risk factors that are associated with them. Some of the common risk factors between erectile dysfunction and heart ailments include the following:

Diabetes: Diabetes or an increase in blood sugar levels is known to impact both issues directly. Men who have diabetes are at a high risk of both erectile dysfunction and heart diseases along with some eye-related problems.

Tobacco use: Tobacco is one of the biggest evils behind erectile dysfunction and heart diseases. Men who have a habit of consuming tobacco in any form have a high risk of both disorders.

High cholesterol: Our body produces two different types of cholesterol – high-density lipoprotein (HDL) or good cholesterol and low-density lipoprotein (LDL) or bad cholesterol. When the levels of LDL increase beyond a limit in the body, it can lead to bad cardiac health. It leads to atherosclerosis, which can bring on erectile dysfunction and heart diseases.

Obesity: Obesity is one of the primary reasons behind poor cardiac health. Excess weight usually worsens the already looming risk of cardiac diseases.

Age: As a person gets older, cardiac health might begin to weaken. Penile erections might take longer than usual. This might not be an indicator of underlying heart disease. However, if these signs exist at a young age, getting your heart scanned to ensure its proper functioning is advisable.

High blood pressure (BP): The impact of high blood pressure on cardiac health is known. If high BP prevails over a long time, it weakens heart muscle by damaging the walls of arteries and the overall vascular system. In turn, this can also impact penile erections, primarily due to the heavy medications usually prescribed by physicians.

Low testosterone: Erectile dysfunction can also happen due to low testosterone count. If the count falls very low, it can impact cardiovascular health as well.

The risks for Erectile Dysfunction and heart diseases can be mitigated by following a healthier lifestyle. A WFPB lifestyle is one of the best ways to do that. It has helped me recover from coronary artery disease and given me the gift of a happy and healthy life.

So far, we have uncovered the different types of heart diseases and the science underlying them. Heart diseases can rise to extreme levels if the right food and lifestyle choices are not made. In the worst cases, they can even lead to death.

I realized this when I came out of my triple bypass operation; I don't recommend it. It sucked in many ways, and I'm never doing that again. As we move forward in the book, I will take you through the lifestyle choices that I made, which helped keep my heart and body fit and healthy. I am confident that incorporating them into your life will give you similar results. Are you ready to transform your lifestyle?

Chapter 3
Debunking Common Myths

Ever since I have adopted a WFPB lifestyle, I have been a regular follower of discussions or information about all things WFPB. Learning about different substitutions, nutritional values, quick tips, and new recipes excite me.

However, some of the discussions seem concerning to me for a myriad of reasons. For instance, I read a blog on the nutritional benefits of a WFPB diet which suggested the users purchase expensive protein-based powders to meet their daily protein requirements. Another told the users only to focus on eating potatoes and legumes for balancing their protein intake.

When it comes to nutrition, it's always hard to know what to trust. With the democratization of information, there is a lot of misinterpretation and misinformation that has hit the world of nutrition. Through this chapter, I intend to provide more context to the world of a WFPB lifestyle while debunking some of the most common myths surrounding it.

Myths Around the WFPB Diet

The world of WFPB nutrition is filled with misconceptions about health benefits, palatability, and safety. Let us check out some of the most common myths and dispel them with credible scientific evidence.

Myth 1: It's just another name for a vegan diet

There isn't a very strict definition of a vegan diet and a plant-based diet. As is evident from the name, a plant-based diet is rich in plant products, but it is more of a lifestyle than just a diet. So is veganism. It goes beyond diet to a philosophy rooted in the rejection of animal commodification, and on a practical level also includes things like boycotting leather clothing. The staples of a plant-based diet are fruits, vegetables, tubers, nuts and seeds, whole grains, and legumes – all in as close to natural form as possible.

Additionally, it is essential to note that a vegan diet might not necessarily be a healthy one. Many highly refined food items get the tick. In fact, there are many vegan-friendly, high-calorie, and low nutrient junk foods available in the market that essentially take away the 'healthy' aspect of a vegan diet. We are coming for you, flavor-laden bags of corn chips!

Myth 2: You can't get complete protein by eating just plants

This is the most common myth in the world of WFPB diets. This age-old myth comes from the idea that plants contain a certain kind of amino acid, and we need to opt for a combination diet to fulfill our protein requirements. However, the word 'complete' is misleading. All WFPB diets contain a complete profile of amino acids. The difference is usually attributed to the amount of essential amino acid per source of WFPB food. This, in turn, determines the quality of the protein source.

Eating enough protein is not as hard as it seems. According to the experts, the recommended daily allowance (RDA) of protein is 0.8 grams per kilogram of body weight. You can figure out your daily intake of protein by multiplying your weight in pounds by 0.36, or for a more accurate RDA of protein based on Dietary Reference Intakes (RDI) use this calculator: http://bit.ly/DRICalculator.

For a 45-year-old woman who weighs 150 pounds and doesn't exercise regularly, would require 54 grams of protein per day. Surprisingly, this usually accounts for around ten percent of someone's daily diet. For most Americans, nearly 16% of their daily calories already come from proteins!

Achieving the RDA while following a WFPB diet is possible with the following food items:

Tofu

Lentils

Seeds

Whole grains

Nuts

Beans

Proteins come from a variety of WFPB foods. The key is to ensure that you are consuming a good combination of varied WFPB foods every day. Eat plants to your heart's desire, and rest assured that you will get more than enough proteins to meet your daily caloric needs.

Myth 3: Eating a WFPB diet will leave you hungry all the time

It is often seen that people are reluctant to switch to a WFPB diet based on their fear of being hungry all the time. Because the caloric density of plants isn't too high, people tend to think such diets can't be fulfilling or satisfying. This is a myth!

WFPB diets are rich in fiber concentration. Food items such as vegetables, legumes, fruits, and whole grains have a very high fiber composition that leaves you feeling full for considerably long durations. The fiber in these food items fills up your stomach and stabilizes your blood sugar levels to prevent food cravings. It is also associated with many other health benefits, such as improved gut health.

So, start your day with a bowl of fruits and oats, pack some baked tofu and your favorite vegetables for lunch and come home to a bean chili dinner. Nothing can get better than this!

Myth 4: There is no proof that a WFPB diet is better than other forms of diet

Scientific studies have been debunking the myth that the WFPB diet is not better than any other form of diet. A WFPB diet cannot only prevent the risk of coronary artery disease (the leading cause of death in men and women) but also cure it.

Dr. Caldwell Esselstyn Jr, MD at Cleveland Clinic, conducted a 21-year study to understand the impact of a WFPB diet on coronary artery disease (CAD) patients. The results of the study revealed that advanced CAD was reversed or stopped in patients who adopted the WFPB diet (strictly whole food, plant-based, no salt, no oil, no sugar) and kept their total cholesterol level under 150 mg/dl with an LDL cholesterol under 80 mg/dl (Esselstyn, 2007).

"Coronary artery disease is virtually absent in cultures that eat WFPB diets, such as the Tarahumara Indians of northern Mexico, the Papua highlanders of New Guinea, and the inhabitants of rural China and central Africa," said Dr. Esselstyn in Preventive Cardiology (Esselstyn, 2001).

Further, a study was conducted in 2008 by Dean Ornish, MD, which showed that a WFPB diet combined with exercise and stress reduction could delay the advancement of prostate cancer in some men (Ornish, 2008).

Such powerful health benefits are seldom seen in any other form of diet. So, enjoy your leguminous salad and stay confident about the magic that it will do to your body!

Myth 5: There is nothing wrong with lean animal protein that is fried or grilled

Scientifically, saturated fats are known to increase the cholesterol levels in the body, thus contributing to an increase in plaquing of your arteries and making you prone to cardiac illnesses. On the other hand, WFPB food items are rich in unsaturated fatty acids (or good fat) that help keep cholesterol levels under control and cardiac disorders at bay.

Usually, it is the cooking method that is more harmful to the body than the meat. When animal products like meat are grilled or fried, they lead to the formation of AGEs or advanced glycation end products. The AGEs are toxins released during frying or grilling and expedite the aging process in the body. This, in turn, causes inflammation and oxidative damage that can lead to health issues such as cataracts, muscular degeneration in the eye, or even Alzheimer's disease. In worst cases, AGEs directly impact the liver, heart, and kidneys, thus leading to reduced longevity.

Compared to the lean meat items, WFPB items with optimum carbohydrate composition such as fruits, vegetables, legumes, and whole grains have fewer AGEs and thus contribute towards enhancing longevity.

Myth 6: WFPB diets are very rich in carbohydrates

Carbohydrates have been associated with weight gain or diabetes for the longest time now. The myth stems from the biological process that converts carbohydrates into blood glucose, thus raising the risk of diabetes.

However, most of this is partial information. WFPB food items such as fruits and vegetables have a balanced composition of all the macronutrients. If they provide carbohydrates, they also offer other macronutrients that aid in the complete digestion and breakdown of carbs and release of energy.

If you keep your portion size, variety, and balance under control, the carbohydrates in your food will be completely broken down, and you won't experience any sudden spike in your blood sugar levels. Controlled sugar levels keep the risk of diabetes at bay.

Myth 7: You shouldn't eat WFPB diets if you are an athlete

One of the most common misconceptions is that a WFPB diet is not suitable for athletes. There is a big worry that if you switch to a WFPB diet, your ability to build muscles and level up athletic activity will suffer.

If that were the case, famous sports icons such as Serena Williams and Tom Brady wouldn't have adopted a WFPB diet. The switch is because a WFPB diet can reduce your recovery time between consecutive workouts by lowering inflammation in the body.

Many people also think that athletic activity becomes slow due to the fewer proteins present in WFPB foods. They also believe that gaining muscle is a challenge with the WFPB diet. It must be understood that more protein doesn't necessarily mean more muscle. If you are adding more protein to your diet without increasing physical exercise, you won't gain muscles. In fact, excessive amounts of proteins can harm your health as well.

Myth 8: A WFPB diet doesn't supply enough vitamins and minerals

This myth is as far away from the truth as possible. Plants are the most nutrient-dense foods that we can consume. For instance, legumes are a rich source of iron, zinc, and calcium. Fruits such as berries are a rich source of vitamin K and manganese, whereas tropical fruits such as mangoes are rich in vitamin C.

It is recommended that vegans and those on a WFPB diet take vitamin B12, since this vitamin is generally not found in fruits and vegetables. Also, consider taking vitamin D if you reside in northern climates due to lower exposure to direct sunlight.

The rule of thumb here is to include as much variety as possible in your diet. Expanding your palette is good for your body and exciting for your taste buds!

Myth 9: It's very expensive!

This is more of an excuse than a myth. After having consumed plant-based products for many years, I can altogether vouch for the budget-friendliness of a plant-based diet.

A plant-based diet focuses mainly on consuming minimally processed foods, so those vegan cheeses and ice creams that burn a hole in the pocket aren't what you will be purchasing. Additionally, since it is about cutting meat from your diet, it will result in huge savings. Did you ever come across a sirloin steak on a restaurant menu that was cheaper than a salad?

Additionally, since your purchase will be focused on fruits, veggies, and legumes, all of these can be found in frozen or canned form. Not only is this a much cheaper option, but you can stock up your pantry and say goodbye to your weekly visit to the market. Fresh fruit and vegetables could be bought seasonally, and grains and legumes can also be purchased dried in bulk. After all, seasonal eatables are also budget-friendly ones! Once you have made the switch and stocked up your favorite plant-based food items in your pantry, you can stay assured about saving plenty!

Myth 10: WFPB diet is boring!

When you switch to a plant-based diet, it can be quite overwhelming initially. This feeling arises because you give up on all your meat items, learn new recipes to cook food made primarily from plant-based products, and try out some new flavors. But new is always interesting, right?

On the other hand, a meat-rich diet is basically a turn of four major items – beef, pork, chicken, and seafood. To these, token vegetables are added to round off the plate. Over time, we tend to start repeating a handful of meals, which can be pretty dull sometimes!

As you learn new recipes while switching to a plant-based lifestyle (PBL), you might even invigorate or rekindle your love for cooking. How can that be boring?

Key takeaways

There are a lot of WFPB nutrition myths buzzing around. The good news is that all of these are myths. Plant-based nutrition is wholesome and delicious. Following a well-rounded WFPB diet can provide you with adequate macronutrients for the effective functioning of your body.

Some of the key takeaways from the myths that we debunked are as follows:

You will get ample amounts of proteins from a WFPB diet without having to consume any additional protein supplements. A WFPB meal is loaded with fibers that satiate your hunger in the most nutritious way.

A well-rounded WFPB diet is cleaner and loaded with goodness. It keeps you fit and healthy.

Lean animal food turns unhealthy on frying or grilling. You don't want that!

WFPB diets provide an adequate amount of carbohydrates to fuel the body effectively. No more, no less.

Athletes are switching to a WFPB diet. Its health benefits attract everyone!

Fruits and vegetables are the most significant source of vitamins and minerals. The only supplement recommended is vitamin B12 and possibly vitamin D, depending on where you live.

It's affordable. Not only will you be able to buy food at reasonable prices, but you can also stock it in efficient quantities in frozen or dried forms, as well as cutting out on your trips to the butcher, thus saving more money.

Myths can crop up everywhere. Just like plant-based nutrition, there are many myths and misconceptions regarding cardiac diseases. In the next section, I will reveal and debunk some of the most common myths regarding the heart's health. Keep reading.

Myths Around Cardiac Diseases

Cardiac diseases are the most common reason for death in the whole world. Globally, nearly 18 million people die due to cardiovascular illnesses representing 32% of all deaths (*Cardiovascular Diseases*, 2019).

According to the Centers for Disease Control and Protection (CDC), one person dies every 36 seconds due to a cardiovascular illness. It accounts for one out of every four deaths in America (*Heart Disease Facts | Cdc.Gov*, 2021).

Even with such statistics, the awareness about the detection and cure of cardiac diseases is meager. This space is laden with many myths and misconceptions that blind people so that they either get scared or give up on the subject altogether.

In this section, I intend to set the record straight and separate facts from fiction, so that we can better tackle cardiovascular illnesses. Let's debunk some of the most common myths together:

Myth 1: Young people don't need to worry about heart diseases

It is an established fact that heart diseases are very likely to affect people over the age of 65. But, of late, between four and ten percent of heart attacks occur in people under 45 years of age. More than half of young adults aged 18-25 have at least 1 coronary heart disease (CHD) risk factor and almost one-quarter have advanced atherosclerotic lesions (Arts et al., 2014). Heart diseases can happen to anyone!

The health of our heart is dependent on many factors. One of the most important factors is how we live our lives as kids, adolescents, and adults. It lays the groundwork for our cardiac health as we age.

For instance, if we eat a diet laden with saturated or trans fats and smoke tobacco frequently, we put ourselves at a very high risk of heart diseases as we age. However, if we make positive changes in our diet and lifestyle very early in life, we lay the foundation for a happy and healthy heart.

Myth 2: Taking cholesterol-lowering drugs allows you to eat whatever you want

Many people who take cholesterol-lowering pills believe that they can eat whatever they want as long as they are taking their medicine. That's not right!

Cholesterol is formed in our body in two ways – either through the food we eat or through biological processes in the liver. Many cholesterol-lowering drugs, like statins, reduce the level of cholesterol in the blood. Statins block an enzyme associated with the production of cholesterol which ultimately lowers the cholesterol levels in the whole body. However, this means that cholesterol can still make it into the blood via the food we eat.

Cholesterol-lowering drugs can only help in overriding the adverse effects of a poor diet. But a poor diet can significantly increase the risk of other cardiac diseases such as hypertension, diabetes, and obesity.

Myth 3: Heart diseases run in my family, so there's nothing that I can do about it

Many people give up on understanding or improving their heart health when they find out that heart diseases run in their families, as it does in my family, afflicting both my father and mother. Understand that this is not the right approach!

If your close family members have experienced heart disease, it could mean that you might also have an increased risk. However, this is not an established fact, and there are many ways in which you can reduce the risk even if there's a genetic susceptibility.

The best way to reduce the risk is to follow a healthy diet, gradually lowering and altogether shunning alcohol and tobacco consumption, introducing daily physical exercise, and managing blood pressure. Following these basic protocols can keep you fit and healthy, even if your family lineage suggests otherwise!

Myth 4: Heart diseases are for men and cancer is for women

Heart diseases don't differentiate between men and women. The leading cause of death among all women in the US remains heart disease. Cancer mostly kills young women to middle-aged women, whereas heart disease primarily kills the very old (Pathak, 2016) .

Men indeed tend to develop heart diseases earlier in life than women and have a greater risk of coronary artery disease or CAD. However, women have a higher risk of stroke.

A paper titled (*Gender Differences in Cardiovascular Disease*, 2019) explains the scenario by saying, "Although the incidence of [cardiovascular disease] in women is usually lower than in men, women have a higher mortality and worse prognosis after acute cardiovascular events."

Myth 5: Coughing during a heart attack can save your life

Many sources claim that coughing vigorously during a heart attack (also known as cough CPR) can save your life. This myth is a misrepresentation of a research paper published nearly 42 years ago.

According to the paper, patients who had a cardiac arrest in the hospital during arteriography and coughed every one to three minutes outlived others by nearly 39 seconds.

However, a heart attack is not the same as cardiac arrest. There is no medical evidence that supports the argument that cough CPR helps during emergency situations like a heart attack. The best approach is to call the emergency services if you suspect you're having a heart issue.

Myth 6: People with heart diseases should totally avoid eating fat

You know that you need to control the intake of fats, especially if you are at risk of or suffering from heart diseases. But the focus should be on eliminating saturated fats usually found in butter, bacon, sausages, and biscuits and trans fats found in baked goods, frozen pizzas, and microwaved popcorn.

However, unsaturated fats can provide many health advantages. Omega-3 is an unsaturated fatty acid that is believed to be good for our heart's health. In a 2017 advisory from the American Heart Association, it was stated that replacing saturated fats with unsaturated fats as part of a healthy diet helps reduce the risk of heart disease (Swap

Saturated Fats with Unsaturated Fats for a Healthy Heart, 2017). A WFPB diet that includes soybeans, tofu, and flaxseeds can provide the necessary omega-3 fatty acids to keep your heart happy and healthy. It should be noted that Dr. Caldwell Esselstyn showed coronary artery disease (CAD) arrest and reversal in a study of 198 patients after placing them on a strict diet including whole grains, legumes, lentils, other vegetables, and fruit, and avoidance of all oils, fish, meats, dairy products, unsaturated fats like avocado and nuts, sugary foods, and excess salt (C. G. Jr. Esselstyn et al., 2014).

Myth 7: Taking multivitamins can prevent heart disease

Vitamins are necessary for our overall health. Although most vitamins, when taken in prescribed quantities, don't impair our heart's health, there is little to no medical evidence that suggests taking vitamin supplements will reduce the risk of heart diseases. They certainly do not replace a healthy diet and regular physical exercise.

According to the experts at (British Heart Foundation, n.d.), "There are no shortcuts when it comes to nutrition — supplements are not a replacement for healthy food. You might be prescribed a vitamin or mineral supplement by a health professional for other reasons, but we do not recommend people take multivitamins to help prevent heart and circulatory diseases."

Key Takeaways

Heart diseases are common, but they are not inevitable. There are many ways of reducing the risk of heart diseases, even if they run in the family lineage. The bottom line here is to stop believing the myths and focus on medical advice.

Some of the key takeaways from the myths that we debunked are as follows:

Heart diseases can happen to anyone, regardless of their age. Don't ignore your heart health, thinking that you are too young to be at risk.

Cholesterol-lowering pills don't eliminate the risk of heart diseases. They only reduce it a little bit.

Heart diseases can be avoided and reversed even if they run in your family lineage. Don't give in to the myths that state otherwise!

Heart diseases can crop up regardless of one's gender.

Your priority during a heart attack should be to call the emergency services instead of focusing on cough CPR.

Some fats are good. Consuming them in a well-balanced diet can keep your heart healthy.

Taking multivitamins isn't a shortcut to achieving good heart health. Consuming a well-balanced diet is.

Pros and Cons of a Plant Based Diet

Every coin has two sides, and so does a WFPB diet. There are many pros and cons of a WFPB diet, and it is vital to understand them to meet your personal and health needs. Rest assured, the number of pros far outweighs the cons.

Pros of WFPB diet

The WFPB diet is low in saturated and trans fats, keeps the cholesterol levels under check, and is rich in vitamins, minerals, and antioxidants. Here's a list of the benefits that a WFPB diet can offer to you:

- It improves your cardiovascular health by keeping blood pressure and heart rate under control
- It lowers the total cholesterol levels and LDL levels
- It helps in effective weight management and lowers body mass index (BMI)
- It reduces the carbon footprint
- It protects against many types of cancers
- It lowers the risk of type II diabetes
- It improves neurocognitive functions
- It helps in the prevention of dementia and Alzheimer's disease
- It improves glycemic control

Cons of a WFPB diet

There are some downsides to a WFPB diet. While these are minimal concerns, it is essential to consider them for a well-rounded understanding. Here's a list of the small flipsides of a WFPB diet:

Meeting the requirement of vitamin B12 can be difficult because it is present in soil and not in plants. You might have to take supplements for it.

Meal planning and preparations are very crucial for staying on track especially in households where not everyone is WFPB.

Changing diets can lead to some temporary side effects, such as flatulence.

Avoiding all animal products can be problematic in the beginning. However, you become more robust, and the cravings for meat disappear over time.

The secret to getting started on a WFPB diet is to keep it simple. Start with small changes and gradually replace animal products with plant foods. Make the choice of staying healthy and stick with it!

Part 2

The Five Healthy Habits

Chapter 4
A Plethora of Consumable Choices: Consume to Your Heart's Content

The health benefits of a WFPB diet are plenty. But while deciding to switch to a WFPB diet, most people are faced with this question: "What can I eat?"

Thankfully, a WFPB diet offers a wide variety of delicious and healthy food items to eat. The focus is on making WFPB food items central to your daily meals. Once you set your pace, you can be as strict with your diet as you want to be.

Let us put the confusion of deciding what whole plant foods to eat at rest and discuss some of the best plant foods you can eat and enjoy.

The Five Essential Food Groups of a WFPB Diet

A WFPB diet has five essential food groups that can provide the body with essential nutrition without compromising taste. Let us go through them one by one:

Fruits: We have all known that a balanced diet is a key to a happy and healthy life. The most critical component of a balanced diet is fruits. Fruits are a rich source of vitamins, minerals, fiber, and even water. Each type of fruit contains varying quantities of these elements and a rich number of antioxidants, polyphenols, and phytochemicals. All these components are essential for the efficient functioning of the human body, and eating fruits is an excellent way of achieving that.

If you are one of those people who are apprehensive about the sugar content of fruits, this will put your concerns to rest: Fruits contain naturally occurring sugars that are good for your body. They don't lead to any harmful effects in the body the way artificial food items do.

It is to be understood that the health benefits of fruits far outweigh the sugar content. Abstaining from eating fruits would lead to the exclusion of essential micronutrients and antioxidants from your diet. Don't fear fruit; savor it!

Vegetables: Vegetables are a wealthy source of vitamins, minerals, dietary fibers, and antioxidants. The green leafy vegetables are loaded with nutrition and have very few calories. Stalk vegetables, such as celery and asparagus, are a rich source of minerals and folic acid. Due to their low-calorie content and high nutritious value, vegetables are a necessity in your everyday life.

The health benefits of consuming vegetables are abundant, making it a perfect meal choice for anyone who wants to lead a healthy lifestyle. If you are one of those people, add vegetables to your diet starting today!

Legumes: Legumes are a well-balanced source of vitamins, fiber, healthy calories, and essential micro and macronutrients. Some legumes even have calcium content equivalent to a glass of milk and other components like essential amino acids, antioxidants, and 'resistance starch,' which help keep the blood sugar levels under control.

There are more than 160,00 varieties of beans and legumes. Some of the most popular ones include chickpeas, peanuts, black beans, lentils, and soybeans. The nutritional benefits of legumes depend upon the quantity consumed. For instance, if you consume half a cup of cooked black beans, you take in 114 calories, 7.6 grams of protein, 20 grams of carbohydrates, and zero fat or cholesterol. So, are you going to let go of all these benefits by not consuming beans and legumes?

Whole grains: Whole grains have been a part of our platters for thousands of years now. And rightly so! They are a vibrant nutrient source that keeps diabetes, high blood pressure, and obesity at bay.

Whole grains are essentially the seeds of grassy plants known as cereals. However, seeds of some non-grass plants are also rich in fiber, such as quinoa and amaranth.

Whole grains are made of three layers, each of which is laden with beneficial components. The first layer is called *bran* and is rich in minerals, antioxidants, and fiber. The second layer is called *endosperm* and is the gold mine of healthy carbohydrates. Finally, the third layer is called the *germ*. This layer is an excellent resource of proteins, vitamins, minerals, and plant compounds. With such a power-packed composition, including whole grains in your diet is a must.

Common whole grains include oatmeal, quinoa, buckwheat, millet, sorghum, and brown rice. Refined grains have the bran and germ removed, which leads to a dip in their nutritional components. Therefore, it is important to include whole grains in your diet to extract the maximum benefits.

Tubers or root vegetables: Tubers or root vegetables are called functional foods. Like the other four food items of the pentavalent, tubers also offer numerous desirable health benefits such as proteins, antioxidants, and energy. Additionally, tubers have a rich composition of water and thus help maintain the body's ionic requirements.

Root vegetables and tubers have a high starch component, so they serve as quick energy resources. The energy component of a root vegetable is one-third of an equivalent quantity of rice or wheat, and the rest of it is moisture content.

Among the tubers, potatoes, sweet potatoes, and yams contain a very high number of proteins. Along with proteins and amino acids, they are also a rich source of micronutrients such as potassium, sulfur, and beta-carotene, all of which are essential for the healthy functioning of the human body. Cutting them out from your diet means letting go of their goodness. Don't commit that sin!

The beauty of a WFPB diet is that you can mix and match the food items and create new platters for yourself every day. However, the focus is on cutting down the consumption of processed or refined food items and enjoying more natural forms of food. So fill your plate with fruits, nuts, vegetables, or any earlier mentioned food items and welcome good health and wellness.

How to Transition to a Whole Food, Plant-Based (WFPB) Lifestyle

If you have never followed a WFPB diet or lifestyle, transitioning to one might look challenging. However, the challenge is only as big as you make it. Although it requires some planning, effort, and willpower initially, once you start enjoying this diet and feel the benefits, there will be no going back.

Here are seven simple strategies to smoothly transition to a WFPB diet without being too hard on yourself:

Start slow: No new change happens instantly. The adoption of a WFPB lifestyle is no different. The key here is to start slow and gradually increase your pace.

Start by picking up a few WFPB meals and rotating them throughout the week. The meals can be anything – fruits, lentil stew, quinoa balls, or whatever you like. You can even start with meals that you have previously enjoyed, such as bean and rice burritos, or jacket potatoes. Then try to build on these meals.

Human beings are creatures of habit. In the case of a WFPB diet, stick to fewer dishes at first and learn the new language of food without feeling the pressure of being perfect.

Cut down the intake of meat and processed food: Don't go cold turkey in the beginning! Start by changing the proportion of plant and animal-based foods on your plate. By doing so, you will accustom your mind to the idea of eating more WFPB food items, and your body will eventually get used to it.

You can start by adding salads and beans to your new diet and reducing the intake of dairy products. Gradually, continue swapping the animal-based items with the WFPB ones in your favorite recipes. For instance, swap soft cheese with tofu or soy and enjoy the new dish!

Commit to one WFPB meal every day: Now that you have made the first step, start committing to at least one WFPB meal every day. This could be breakfast, lunch, or dinner. A good WFPB breakfast could be a good start.

Try out new recipes to prepare a delicious WFPB meal that pleases your palate. Eventually, work on getting accustomed to a plant-based lunch and then dinner. It might be difficult at first, but it will surely be worth it.

Watch your protein: Protein overconsumption is a widespread phenomenon noticed in people switching to a plant-based diet. The average protein requirement is 0.8 grams per kilogram (2.2 pounds) of our body weight. Many people focus on doubling or even tripling the recommended protein intake in their quest to provide enough protein to the body. The trend is seen primarily in people trying to bulk up and gain muscles.

Overdoing it is wrong. Proteins are good for our body but overconsuming them can have specific side effects. All the plant foods contain enough amounts of amino acids in varying quantities. A proper mix and match of various WFPB food items can help us meet all our requirements with ease.

As long as we can eat enough calories to sustain our daily bodily functions by focusing on protein-rich plant foods cutting down on refined foods, we won't become deficient in protein at all.

Know your food: You need to understand how to make your food taste healthy and delicious without compromising its nutritional aspect. It is crucial to stick to items that keep the nutritional goodness intact.

In addition to this, it is imperative to educate yourself on the nutritional requirements of your body and the nutritional composition of various ingredients that you consume. It will help you know what a balanced diet means in your case and how you can achieve good health. The Physicians Committee for Responsible Medicine has established the nutritional requirements throughout the life cycle. In its 2020 nutritional guide for Clinicians, it states "a renewed emphasis on vegetables, fruits, whole grains, and legumes can help prevent weight problems and chronic illnesses, including cardiovascular disease, diabetes, and cancer, among others. Plant-based diets meet or exceed recommended intakes of most nutrients and have the advantage of being lower in total fat, saturated fat, and cholesterol than typical Western diets (Physicians Committee for Responsible Medicine, 2020)

Stock up on healthy foods: We can feel hungry any time. The probability of eating unhealthy or processed food items increases multifold during such occasions. To prevent that from happening, it is essential for you to stock up on healthy foods.

This might include delicious items such as kale chips, dairy-free milk, tofu, and tempeh, to suit your palate. Keep them in your bag, kitchen, drawers, or any place where you could reach out when you suddenly feel hungry.

Keep your meals fun and exciting: A WFPB diet doesn't have to be boring. There are many delicious yet easy recipes to explore for every meal of the day.

If you are not a kitchen expert, start by cooking more straightforward recipes. For instance, stir some veggies and beans in a pan, add sauce, season with salt and pepper and enjoy a delicious bowl of soup.

Additionally, don't bore yourself with the same recipes every time. If you feel like eating a dessert, whip up a dessert with plant-based ingredients and treat yourself with taste. As you start enjoying the new foods, you will start noticing the health benefits that they bring and start craving a whole WFPB food item!

Don't be hard on yourself as you transition to a plant-based diet. Take baby steps and slowly find your way. Transitions take time.

Sample Shopping List and Meal Plan:

I know you might need help curating the right shopping list while starting your experimentation with a WFPB diet. Here's a sample shopping list that offers you suggestions that you can follow as you start. Gradually, make a shopping list that suits your taste.

Fruits: Fruits are essential. Include pineapples, grapes, apples and citrus fruits like oranges, grapefruits and fibrous fruits like mangoes, and avocados in your list.

Dark, leafy vegetables: Kale, spinach, bok choy, arugula are must-haves.

Whole grains: Include grains like quinoa, barley, brown rice in your list.

Dried or canned legumes: You might want to cook something for yourself quickly. For these situations, pick up canned lentils, chickpeas, and black beans. Tofu and tempeh. Tahini sauce.

Non-dairy milk: (oats, almond, soy) for your sudden dessert cravings.

Nuts and seeds: like walnuts, chia seeds, almonds to snack upon.

Meal plan:

Shifting to a WFPB diet can be challenging. But with creative meal plans to try, you can make the shift with some ease.

Here is a five-day WFPB diet plan that you can try. The program is not set in stone; you can always make changes as per your taste. But it will serve as an excellent start to your journey.

Day 1

Breakfast: Avocado toast on a slice of oil-free sour dough bread; 1 cup of fresh berries

Lunch: 1 3/4 cup red curry lentil soup with kale

Dinner: 1 serving Mediterranean quinoa-stuffed peppers; 2 grilled tofu kebabs

Day 2

Breakfast: 1 1/2 cups tofu scramble with sautéed veggies and a pinch of turmeric

Lunch: 1 Mediterranean veggie wrap (omit feta; substitute hummus)

Dinner: 1 serving Indian potato and lentil stew; 1 cup cooked basmati rice

Day 3

Breakfast: Mango banana breakfast smoothie (substitute plant milk)

Lunch: 1 cup Southwest quinoa salad

Dinner: 2 poblano portobello mushroom tacos; 1 serving blue corn chips; 1/4 cup fresh salsa

Day 4

Breakfast: 1 cup oatmeal topped with nuts and bananas

Lunch: 1 cup dairy-free corn chowder; 1 1/2 cups kale and cranberry salad

Dinner: 1 serving maple-roasted root vegetables

Day 5

Breakfast: 1-2 slices vegan zucchini bread; 8 ounces fresh orange juice

Lunch: 1 cup creamy broccoli soup (try white cannellini beans instead of dairy); 1 cup of spring mix greens tossed with radishes, cucumbers, fresh herbs

Dinner: 1 serving chili and lime roasted meatless Buddha bowl

WFPB Beginner Recipe Websites

Are you ready to get cooking? Here are eight of my favorite websites to get easy to prepare whole food plant-based recipes for beginners.

Forks Over Knives (Forksoverknives.com)

This is one of the first websites people frequently stumble across when they explore the realm of plant-based diets, as it comes from the makers of the popular documentary of the same name. FOK's blog features over 250 free vegan recipes from a variety of well-known vegan recipe blogs, as well as their own cookbook.

Chef AJ (ChefAJ.com)

Are you attempting to lose weight? Chef AJ is for you. Chef AJ has four decades of expertise as a celebrity plant-based chef and pioneer, helping people achieve their weight loss goals with delicious plant-based SOS-free (no salt, no oil, no sugar) meals and her Ultimate Weight Loss Program.

Mama Sezz (MammaSezz.com)

Whether it's through their ready-made meals or free plant-based recipes, MammaSezz is committed to making eating whole food plant-based simple. Every week, Chef Caroline prepares plant-based cuisine for various palates, ranging from dairy-free cheesecake to vegan pesto-stuffed mushrooms.

Happy Herbivore (HappyHerbivore.com)

Lindsay S. Nixon, aka the Happy Herbivore, is a great recipe resource for weight loss and families. She specializes in low-fat vegan foods that are both economical and simple to prepare.

Clean Food Dirty Girl (CleanFoodDirtyGirl.com)

The go-to for whole food plant-based meal preparation, and she does so with a sense of humor. This is the ideal alternative for anyone who enjoys cooking and wants to do it the whole food plant-based way, with a seemingly limitless array of plant-based recipes and meal plans (both free and for purchase).

Straight Up Food (StraightUpFood.com)

Another great resource for those looking to cut salt, oil, and sugar from their diet. All WFPB recipes here are SOS-free, with gluten-free options as well.

Running on Real Food (RunningonRealFood.com)

This is not just a diet; it's a lifestyle and Running on Real Food is just that. This is the vegan food blog if you're looking for healthy meals to charge your active lifestyle.

Nutriciously (Nutriciously.com)

Alena and Lars founded Nutriciously to show people how simple (and delicious) it is to consume a plant-based diet. Their website contains a ton of delicious vegan recipes to try at home, as well as some helpful advice and suggestions for plant-based newbies, such as how to eat this way when travelling and how to handle difficult family conversations.

Supplementation Requirement on a WFPB Diet

One widespread concern that people have while switching to a WFPB diet is that it may not provide the necessary vitamins and minerals for the body. While a WFPB diet is mainly self-sufficient, here is a list of nutrients that you might need to supplement with while following this diet:

Vitamin B12

Vitamin B12 is largely found in soils. The foods usually regarded as B12 rich include unwashed organic produce, nori, spirulina, and mushrooms grown in B12-rich soils.

Since vitamin B12 is essential for the effective functioning of the human body, such as protein metabolism and transport of oxygen-containing cells across the body, it is vital to maintain its daily requirement.

The daily recommended intake of vitamin B12 is 2.4 mcg per day for adults, 2.6 mcg during pregnancy, and 2.8 mcg while breastfeeding.

The best way to meet these requirements is either by consuming B12-fortified food items like soy products or plant milk or by taking vitamin B12 supplements.

Vitamin B12 is best absorbed in small doses. Thus, the less frequently you take in B12, the more quantity you will have to take.

Vitamin D

Your body needs an adequate amount of vitamin D to absorb calcium and phosphorus from the gut effectively. It is also essential for immune functioning, memory, and muscle recovery.

The Institute of Medicine set the recommended daily allowance (RDA) at 600 to 800 IU. Official recommendations range from 200 IU a day to 10,000 IU daily. Although there is research that shows taking 10,000 IU everyday can lead to toxicity. Therefore, a safe recommended dose of vitamin D to get us to the purported optimal level is 2,000 IU (Faclm, 2019).

Since very few food items contain vitamin D, it is usually consumed via supplements. But before taking the supplements, it is advised to get your blood levels tested for vitamin D. If the deficiency can be met by short periods of sun exposure every day, you can skip the supplements. But if it requires you to consume the supplements, you should opt for vitamin D2 pills.

Long-chain omega-3s

Omega 3 fatty acids are crucial for the healthy functioning of our body. Essentially, these fatty acids can be divided into two categories:

Essential omega-3 fatty acids: Alpha-linolenic acid (ALA) is the only essential omega-3 fatty acid, and you can only get it from your diet.

Long-chain omega-3 fatty acids: This omega 3 fatty acids category includes eicosatetraenoic acid (EPA) and docosahexaenoic acid (DHA). These are not called essential because your body can make them from ALA.

Your body needs an adequate amount of omega-3s for effective brain-and-eye coordination. It is also vital to reduce the risk of depression, inflammation, and attention deficit.

The daily recommended intake of omega-3s is 200 mg per day for everyone. You can achieve this intake by supplementing with algae oil (if you are heart-healthy). You can also accomplish this by taking one to two tablespoons of flaxseed meal or chia seeds daily.

Plant-based items with a high ALA content include flax seeds, chia seeds, walnuts, hemp seeds, and soybeans. Getting enough ALAs would help in maintaining healthy levels of EPA and DHA.

Iron

Your body requires red blood cells (RBCs) and DNA to sustain itself. Iron is a nutrient used to make new RBCs and DNA as well as for effective energy metabolism. Iron deficiency can lead to anemia or decreased immune function.

The daily recommended intake of iron is 8 mg for adult men and post-menopausal women. Adult women need 18 mg iron per day, and pregnant women require 27 mg of iron per day.

To achieve the daily requirement, your focus should be on consuming more iron-rich foods such as leafy vegetables, beans, dried fruits, and nuts. You can also explore iron-fortified food items such as cereals, plant milk, and enriched loaves of bread.

Before opting for iron supplements, it is advised to get your heme levels checked by a medical practitioner. If there exists a considerable deficiency, then opt for supplements. If the deficiency can be met by eating iron-rich food items, it is wiser to opt for that and avoid the unnecessary side effects.

Calcium

Good health of teeth and bones is possible only if your body maintains optimum levels of calcium. It also complements muscle functioning, heart health, and nerve signaling.

The daily recommended intake of calcium is 1000 mg per day for most adults and increases to 1200 mg per day for adults above the age of 50.

To achieve the daily requirement, your focus should be on consuming more WFPB sources such as turnip greens, water chestnuts, kale, bok choy, or mustard greens. You can also explore calcium-fortified food items such as cereals, plant milk, or juices.

If your daily calcium intake is below 525 mg, you are at a high risk of bone weakness and fractures. Consuming natural calcium-rich food items is essential. If you are unable to meet the requirement, opting for calcium supplements is a good idea.

Zinc

Zinc is a vital mineral for the repair of body cells, immune health, and effective metabolism. Deficiency of zinc can lead to hair loss, dementia, or delayed healing of wounds.

The daily recommended intake of zinc is 8-11 mg per day for adults and post-menopausal women. Pregnant women require 11-12 mg of zinc per day, and lactating women need 12-14 mg of zinc every day.

Zinc has an active phytate component that limits zinc absorption in the body. For this reason, it is advisable to consume 1.5 times the daily recommendation for effective absorption.

Eating WFPB food items such as whole grains, legumes, nuts, sprouted beans, and fermented items such as tempeh or miso can help meet the recommended levels of zinc.

If you still cannot meet the requirement, you can opt for taking zinc gluconate or a zinc citrate supplement daily. It will provide nearly 50-60% of your daily recommended zinc levels.

Iodine

Your thyroid glands control your metabolism. For a strong metabolism, your body requires an adequate amount of iodine. The deficiency of iodine can lead to hypothyroidism. Lack of iodine during pregnancy or early infancy could lead to irreversible intellectual disability in children.

The daily recommended intake of iodine for adults is 150 mcg per day. Pregnant women should aim for 220 mcg per day, while lactating mothers are recommended to further increase their daily intake of iron to 290 mcg per day.

The only source of iodine for the followers of a WFPB diet is iodized salt. Generally, half a teaspoon (2.5 mL) of salt is enough to get iodine for the day.

If you are not willing to consume iodized salt, you can opt for iodine supplements.

Well-planned WFPB diets can fulfill all your nutritional requirements. But requirements for certain minerals or vitamins like vitamin B12 or vitamin D can only be met with supplements or fortified foods.

Before taking any supplement, it is highly recommended that you visit your healthcare practitioner and get your vitamin or nutrient levels tested. The tests might reveal that you don't require any supplements!

Chapter 5
Stress Silently Kills; What Kills the Killer?

We live in a very fast-paced world that keeps changing every day. Change always creates stress, especially when it is out of one's control. It can be due to anything: moving to a new place, getting started on a new project, or even a surprise birthday party! While you can't always control your circumstances, you can always control how you respond to them.

When stress starts becoming overwhelming or sticks around for a long time, it starts to hamper your well-being. That's when you know that there's a need to knock it out of your life. While there is no one-size-fits-all approach to fighting stress and anxiety, a mix of many positive changes can help relieve yourself from the pangs of stress.

This chapter aims to familiarize you with what stress is and how you can detect and handle it. After all, the first step to managing stress is to recognize it.

Recognizing Stress

Stress has become a part of everyone's daily life. But sometimes, we get so caught up in the flow of life that we fail to recognize stress. As a result, we feel stressed due to stressors that are usually beyond our control. Stressors can be anything: Losing your job, not getting along with a family member, or hating your work.

The way we respond to these stressors determines our stress reactions. Therefore, stress reactions can be different for different people, even if the situation is similar. For instance, while moving to a new city might be exciting for you, it might be a very stressful situation for someone else.

Physiologically, stress happens first in our minds. But its strong effect can have a severe impact on our physical, mental, and emotional well-being. Stress has a great potential to negatively impact our heart health. Sudden, intense stress has the potential to lead to a heart attack. However, when stress and anxiety prevail over a long time (multiple months or years), it leads to chronic stress.

Chronic stress increases the risk of coronary heart disease (CHD) and poor cardiovascular prognosis. It is also associated with increased inflammation (SAGE Journals, 2006). Acute or short-term stress can lead to short-lived events of coronary heart disease. In addition, it leads to an increase in inflammatory markers in the body and an increased risk of events like a heart attack which can be fatal if severe.

Recognizing your stress reactions

Stress is subjective, so are the stress reactions. Every person responds differently to stress and can exhibit different responses to it. Let's look at some common stress responses you may experience.

Thoughts:
Do you have thoughts of sadness all the time?
Do you think about worst case scenarios often?
Does your concentration span decrease?

Emotions:
Do you feel anxious all the time and want to avoid socializing with people?
Do you become extra sensitive to criticism?
Do you feel a lack of self-esteem or confidence?
Do you feel a lack of motivation to do your daily tasks?
Are you angry or frustrated without any specific reason?

Body:
Do you feel a continuous body ache?
Are your muscles tighter and stiffer?
Does your breathing pattern change?
Does your sleeping pattern become abrupt?
Does your heart start pounding very fast?
Do you feel hungry all the time?
Does your mouth dry up?
Have you become prone to minor accidents due to lack of attention?
Do you feel that your thoughts have become rather vague?

Behavior:

Do you stop exercising or going to the gym?

Do you start consuming alcohol or increase its intake?

Do you become nervous?

If your answer to most of the above questions is a yes or you have deviated from your usual way of being, you may be stressed.

On carefully noticing all these questions, you will see that all of them point to a connection between your mind and body. While your mind is the origination point for stress, it impacts your whole body, including your cardiovascular health.

Recognizing stress might not always be easy. It might be relatively more straightforward for others to realize stress in you, but not very clear for you to notice it. Many times, people think that the symptoms are short-lived and will go away. However, you can easily fall prey to chronic stress and anxiety by not paying attention to the early signs.

Managing Stress

Stress management is different for different people. Mostly, it depends on the stressors. Sometimes, changing or removing the stressor helps in effectively managing stress. For instance, you can switch from a hectic and stressful job, or you can change your work schedule.

While removing the stressor is plausible in some cases, it is challenging to do so in many other situations. In such cases, the best solution is to change your stress response. Here are some strategies that can help you in effectively managing stress:

1. **Mental response**: Attitude is everything. While you might not be able to control everything in life, you can always control the way you respond to situations. Most of us have "stress habits" that can make the problem worse than it already is. These habits could be different for different people. Here are some everyday habits observed in some people who are experiencing stress in their lives:

Thinking negatively about a situation even without closely looking at all the facts

Overlooking the good in every case and only focusing on things that can go wrong

Worrying about problems that aren't even theirs to worry about

You need to identify your stress habits. Once you know how you mentally respond to stressful situations, you can work on getting out of your negative stress habits.

2. **Emotional response**: Our emotions control our mood. To effectively manage stress, you need to recognize your emotional response to stress and talk about it. Some common emotional responses seen in people are as follows:

Anxiety: Acute stress leads to anxiety in many people. It isn't just a feeling of sadness but a feeling of overwhelming dread. A study (Fan et al., 2015) found that people who experience high levels of work stress are more likely to have feelings of anxiety or depression.

The best way of dealing with anxiety is to reach out to a mental health professional. One method employed is to take you through guided sessions to get rid of anxiety. You can also fight stress and anxiety by staying active, quitting alcohol or smoking, and following a healthy diet.

Anger and irritability: Irritability and anger are two of the very common emotional responses of people under stress. A National Institutes of Health study found that stress and a feeling of rage are interrelated. The (National Institutes of Health, 2014) also said that higher levels of anger could increase mental stress and the possibility of a stress-related heart attack.

The best way of dealing with feelings of anger or irritability is to practice relaxation techniques. For example, breathing deeply, slow yoga exercises, or simply chanting the word 'relax' can help calm yourself down. In addition to this, you can also opt for techniques like cognitive restructuring.

As a part of cognitive restructuring, you simply change the way you think. For instance, instead of calling a situation frustrating, try calling it a challenging situation that will get better soon. Such thoughts start manifesting, and you get a more balanced perspective that keeps anger at bay.

Memory and concentration problems: Stress has the power of creating concentration problems. It is also believed that certain hormones released during a stressful event can impair your memory.

The best way of keeping away memory impairment during stressful situations is to make positive changes in your lifestyle. For example, maintaining a healthy diet, quitting alcohol and cigarettes, or simply indulging in brain exercises like solving a puzzle can help fight stress.

3. **Physical response:** Stress can make you give up on your physical health. In such a situation, it is very important to engage in some form of physical activity like exercises or light yoga. Regular exercise can help in lifting your mood and serve as a distraction from worries. This practice helps in breaking out of the cycle of negative thoughts that otherwise feed stress.

When you engage in rhythmic exercises like walking, running, or swimming mindfully, you tend to focus on physical sensations in your body as you move. These exercises help in shifting your focus from worries to the progress that your body makes. Regularity in rhythmic movements can relieve you of stress quickly.

4. **Behavioral response**: When you have identified your stressor, it is time to consider reversing its impact. For instance, if your current job makes you stressed, perhaps it's time to switch to a newer job or change your work schedule.

The question of what and how much to change can only be answered by you. Ask yourself what you want to change. How much change is too much change? You can only bring change once you set a goal. So it is essential to set a goal for each change you want to bring in your life.

There is no doubt that change can be challenging, especially in the case of lifestyle changes. Therefore, it is crucial to tackle one change at a time, so you're not overwhelmed. This practice has helped many people in bringing positive lifestyle changes. It will help you too!

WFPB Foods to Reduce Stress and Anxiety

When most people hear the phrase "You are what you eat," they immediately relate it with their own physical health or body size. But research has found that our food choices also impact our mental and emotional health.

A plant-based diet that includes fruits, vegetables, beans, legumes, whole seeds, or nuts contains many specific nutrients and minerals that help fight stress and promote happy mental health. The body easily absorbs the raw vitamins and minerals in these WFPB food items and utilizes these nutrients to fight stress, just the way nature intended it to.

Your focus should be on making the "Big Five" nutrients part of your daily routine. They will help you feel better than any processed food item and are relatively inexpensive, which reduces stress on a whole other level!

Some plant-based food items that can reduce stress and anxiety are as follows:

Spinach

Spinach is laden with the goodness of calcium, potassium, magnesium, iron, and vitamins A and B. These nutrients help in calming the mind and boosting energy levels, all at once. So, whip up a spinach smoothie for your morning drink or add it to your lunch salad, and feel the positive changes yourself. If you are not a fan of spinach, you can try kale instead.

Sweet potatoes

Sweet potatoes are a comfort food laden with nature's goodness. They are rich in magnesium, potassium, calcium, and vitamin B6. If the word 'sweet' in sweet potato worries you about the sugar content, you can put your worries to rest. Despite being sweet, sweet potatoes actually may help lower your glycemic index and halt your cravings quickly, thus preventing you from over-eating. So, pan roast your sweet potatoes and enjoy the sweet delicacy while getting rid of your stress or anxiety.

Chia seeds

If any food deserves the title of stress-releasing superfood, it's chia seeds! Chia seeds are laden with potassium, magnesium, calcium, and even iron and fiber. These seeds don't just reduce stress but also improve your heart's health. If you engage in workouts frequently, chia seeds can help in post-workout recovery while helping you get that lean muscle you have always been dreaming of! Mix some chia seeds in the next smoothie, oatmeal, or pudding that you make and enjoy a delicious, healthy, stress-reducing delicacy!

Cacao

Cacao is a double booster food item. Not only is it rich in calcium, potassium, magnesium, and vitamin B, but it is also laden with tryptophan that activates our feel-good hormones – serotonin and dopamine. These improve your mood and lower stress levels, all while boosting your energy levels! Of course, if you wish to consume cocoa powder instead of cacao directly, you can always do that. However, raw cacao is seven times richer in antioxidants than cocoa powder. So make your favorite pudding today and add cacao or cocoa powder to it to enjoy a healthy and delicious meal.

Banana

Bananas are the easiest fruits to eat, right? Just peel off the yellow skin and enjoy the sweet, creamy, and soft goodness underneath it. But bananas are so much more than just creamy food. They are a rich source of magnesium, potassium, fiber, natural sugars, and vitamin B6. In addition to this, bananas also contain tryptophan, which helps lift your mood and relieve stress or anxiety. You can have bananas in a smoothie or some yummy porridge alongside some nuts and grains. All it takes is peeling the skin off!

It is easy to say that you don't have time to prepare a healthy meal for yourself. But if you spare a few minutes every day to prepare a wholesome WFPB meal for yourself, the benefits will completely amaze you.

Meditation and Prayer to Reduce Stress

Stress creates a fight or flight response in our bodies. Our breathing pace can increase during these responses, blood pressure can shoot up, and heart rate can race. Therefore, it is essential to manage and reduce stress before it becomes chronic. Even when stress is chronic, taking simple measures and engaging in activities such as meditation and prayer can help in reducing it.

Researchers have discovered that meditation produces many positive changes in our bodies (Wallace & Benson, 1972). Some of the most common changes brought about by meditation are as follows:

Controlled heart rate

Lowered stress or anxiety levels

Altered levels of melatonin and serotonin, both regulate functions in the body like mood, sleep, and appetite

Boost in immune response

Reduced usage of external antidepressants or medications

Practicing meditation is easy and inexpensive. You do not require any special equipment for meditating. All you need is a quiet corner in your room or any place you prefer and a few minutes to meditate. It can help in restoring your calm and peace.

Benefits of meditation

Meditation can bring positive changes in your overall well-being. It instills a sense of calm and peace that will keep your energies high and reduce stress levels. These benefits aren't just experienced while you meditate; they continue to make you feel better throughout the day.

Meditation helps in lowering the already built-up information overload that contributes to stress. In addition to this, it also brings many emotional benefits such as:

Developing a positive perspective towards stressful situations

Increasing tolerance levels

Boosting patience and self-awareness

Living in the present.

Building skills that help in tackling stress

Increasing creativity and imagination powers

The benefits of meditation aren't just limited to emotional well-being. Meditation also helps in managing symptoms of physical illnesses such as:

Asthma

Depression

Anxiety

High blood pressure

Disturbed bowel movements

Sleep problems like insomnia

Cancer

Chronic body pain

Heart diseases

Tension headaches

cervical problems

Before you start meditating, it is important to consult your doctor to talk about the pros and cons of the meditation form you will use. While meditation is a very effective way of being healthy, it can't replace traditional medical treatment for diseases. For the same reason, timely consultation with your doctor is essential to fight illnesses.

Types of meditations

Meditation is an umbrella term that describes many ways of achieving relaxed well-being. There are many forms of meditation techniques that you can follow to achieve your goals. Some of these techniques are:

Guided meditation: In this form of meditation, you tend to form mental images of places or situations that you find mentally soothing or relaxing. For this reason, this form of meditation is also called guided visualization.

You can use as many senses as you want, such as smell, touch, or sound. In the beginning, you may need the assistance of a guide or teacher. As you learn the process, you can gradually carry out the meditation process on your own.

Mantra meditation: As is evident from the name, this form of mediation requires you to continuously chant a relaxing mantra or word to prevent distracting thoughts. Usually, meditation mantras are intended to release calming energies and vibes that soothe your mental well-being.

Mindfulness meditation: This form of meditation requires you to be aware and mindful of the situations around you. The purpose of this meditation is "to live in the present moment."

The focus of this form of meditation is to broaden your conscious awareness by focusing on what you experience while meditating. For example, you focus on your breath, observe your thoughts, and let them pass without judgments.

Tai chi: This is a very famous gentle martial art that originated in China. In this form of meditation, you gracefully perform a self-paced series of postures while focusing on your breath.

Qi Gong: Pronounced as "chee-gong," this practice is a balanced combination of relaxation, breathing exercises, meditation, and physical movement that helps in calming the nerves and relieving stress.

Yoga: Originating in India, this practice includes focusing on your breath while performing a series of postures at your own pace. Yoga brings calmness in the mind and flexibility in the body while also improving concentration levels.

Meditation takes practice. You will not become a master on day one, but you can definitely become a master one day with constant practice. It is very common for your mind to wander elsewhere during meditation. Instead of worrying about it, try to slowly bring your mind back to an object or sensation, wherever you originally placed your focus. Once you become a regular at meditating, you will notice its positive impact on your overall well-being.

Chapter 6
Get Up Off Your Duff

"You should exercise daily; it's good for you." We come across this advice time and again in our lives. It is no secret that leading a healthy and active lifestyle is good for your overall health. If you are active and regularly get exercise, you are less likely to develop chronic illnesses, especially heart diseases like coronary artery disease (CAD). You will also be able to live your years with a higher quality of life compared to those who aren't active.

If there is one thing that every patient with CAD should look forward to achieving, it is cardiovascular fitness. It does not matter if you are 50 or 80 years of age; there is always room for improvement. If you have CAD and see no hope left in your life, give yourself a chance to live longer by exercising daily and taking care of your health.

Moderate exercise can do wonders for an individual suffering from CAD. Many people think that a healthy, active lifestyle should only be the top priority of people with illnesses or simply anyone who is above a certain age. If you are one of those people, think again. An active lifestyle is beneficial for everyone regardless of their age or gender. It is a mix of healthy lifestyle choices like eating clean, exercising daily, and meditation that makes one fit and active.

You should not ignore your fitness goals just because you are affected by a particular health condition. Instead of thinking that you are incapable of exercising or following an active lifestyle, it is time to be more motivating and prove yourself wrong. A little effort on your part will go a long way in reshaping your life for the better.

To help motivate you further, here are some benefits of incorporating regular exercise into our daily lives:

Physical fitness and cardiovascular fitness go hand in hand

For the longest time, many scientific reports have examined the relationship between physical fitness and cardiovascular health. These reports, published by institutions like the Centers for Disease Control and Prevention (CDC) and the American Heart Association (AHA), have reinforced a positive relationship between heart health and an active lifestyle. The prevailing view in these reports is that fitter or active individuals tend to develop fewer coronary heart diseases (CHD) than their sedentary counterparts (Myers, 2003). Even if CHDs occur in active individuals in the later stages of life, the impact is relatively less severe.

An active lifestyle is known to reduce the major risk factors that can lead to cardiovascular diseases. Reducing these factors decreases the possibility of a heart attack or stroke, which ultimately reduces the need to go through a coronary revascularization procedure such as bypass surgery or coronary angioplasty.

The significant benefits of regular exercise on cardiovascular health are as follows:

Increase in exercise tolerance
Increase in HDL or good cholesterol
Decrease in LDL or bad cholesterol
Reduction in body weight
Reduction in events of blood pressure increase or decrease
Increase in insulin sensitivity

In addition to these benefits, there are many physiological benefits that regular exercise can provide. For example, you can experience improvements in muscular strength and function, enhancements in your body's ability to take in and use oxygen, and an overall decrease in fatigue and lethargy.

In fact, regular cardiovascular activity is associated with a lower risk of developing diabetes mellitus type 2 (Gill, 2012). Moreover, exercise is known to reduce anxiety and put an end to stress. It also helps in improving the quality of sleep, which in turn improves reactions and energy levels throughout the day.

Coronary atherosclerosis can be reversed with regular exercise

Atherosclerosis is the enemy of good health, and it is becoming increasingly common these days. In this condition, the arteries get clogged by cholesterol that sticks to their walls. This deposition of cholesterol is called plaque and it can eventually slow or block the transport of blood to meet your body's needs. This blockage is called atherosclerosis.

Fighting atherosclerosis is possible with regular exercise. Regular aerobic exercise leads to a reduction in the amount of fat (or bad cholesterol) in the blood, lowers the blood pressure and controls your weight. It also prevents the deposition of plaque and makes the blood flow swifter and smoother across the body.

If you are just a beginner, start with brisk walking, swimming, or bicycling. It is okay to start slow and gradually work up to at least 30-45 minutes of exercising for four to five days in a week. It is advisable to consult your doctor to know about the right exercise routine for you to follow.

You live longer when you exercise regularly

All of us want to live longer, but very few of us do something about it. Having an active lifestyle with appropriate levels of daily exercise is very important to add longevity to your life.

A retrospective study explored the association between long-term mortality and different levels of cardiorespiratory fitness (Mandsager, 2018). The study revealed that not exercising frequently increases your risk of premature death more than cardiovascular diseases or even diabetes.

While any amount of exercise is beneficial for the body, the more you exercise, the greater the benefits. According to an epidemiologist at the American Cancer Society, people who exercise for nearly 450 minutes every week have a 37% lower risk of premature death compared to those who do not exercise at all (Crouch, 2019).

To live longer, you need to exercise regularly. Find a partner and start small. You will slowly get accustomed to an active lifestyle and welcome the beautiful health gifts it offers.

Improve your mood with exercise

Physical activity has the power to improve your mood. How? When you exercise, your brain releases chemicals called endorphins. These endorphins interact with the receptors in your brain and reduce pain, leaving you feeling euphoric. This is where the term "runner's high" originated.

In addition to this, exercise has also proven to fight depression. A Journal of American Medical Association (JAMA) study revealed that as little as 15 minutes of high-intensity exercise could protect people from falling into depression (Harvard Health, 2019). From a less scientific lens, regular exercising can bring more confidence and equip you with a sense of accomplishment.

Enhanced brain functions are a gift of regular exercising

Our brains require a constant supply of oxygen to function up to their full potential. When you engage in high-intensity exercise, your heart rate increases, which pumps oxygen into your brain. The more oxygenated your brain is, the better it will function.

Research by experts at the University of British Columbia revealed that exercising regularly can increase the size of the hippocampus in our brain (Brinke & Bolandzadeh, 2014). This part of the brain controls verbal memory and learning. With an increased or a healthy hippocampus, you will be alert and taking down mental notes of everything around you.

An active lifestyle is a boon for a healthy body. Make exercise a part of your daily routine and march towards a fitter body. Invest in your health and happiness and welcome a better quality of life!

Chapter 7
Breathing Proof

Breathe in. Breathe out. We do this all day, even without thinking about it. Breathing is one of the greatest gifts of our life. At the same time, it is also one of the gifts that we have taken for granted.

Breathing affects our respiratory, neurological, cardiovascular, muscular, gastrointestinal, and psychological health. While it has great significance in our lives, when was the last time you took a deep breath? Deep breathing is not just relaxing; it also positively affects the heart, the brain, the digestive system, the immune system, and maybe even the expression of genes.

According to a physician at Cleveland Clinic's Center for Integrative Medicine, breathing can profoundly impact our physiology and overall health (Cuda, 2010). He says, "You can influence asthma; you can influence chronic obstructive pulmonary disease; you can influence heart failure. There are studies that show that people who practice breathing exercises and have those conditions – they benefit."

Deep breathing comes with a variety of health benefits, both mental and physiological. It is an effective method of controlling stress levels, which controls many coronary heart diseases. Let us take a detailed look at how effective breathing can help in healthy living.

Benefits of Deep Breathing

In a fast-paced world where stopping to take a deep breath seems like a luxury, it might seem more difficult than ever to find peace of mind and keep away stress. However, feeling calm, composed, and at peace is easier than you think. All that you need to do is practice deep breathing. If you are wondering about how it can impact your health and overall lifestyle, take a look at the following benefits of deep breathing:

Reduced anxiety and depression

Mental health problems like anxiety and depression are on the rise in today's society. As the stressors of everyday life take a toll on people's mental health, more and more people are seeking a reliable remedy for fighting these issues.

Deep breathing has been known to alleviate stress levels and improve our mental health tremendously. According to a study by Dr. Chris Streeter, people who have depressive disorders who carried out deep breathing along with daily yoga for a 12-week period saw a massive reduction in the symptoms of depression (Valvano, 2018).

Stress and breathing are interconnected. When you breathe deeply, it slows down the release of a stress hormone called cortisol. The suppression of the hormone reduces the symptoms of anxiety and depression. In addition to this, deep breathing also encourages full oxygen exchange – optimal inhaling of oxygen and exhalation of carbon dioxide. This process slows down the heartbeat and lowers or stabilizes blood pressure, thus decreasing the issues of stress and anxiety.

Decreased pain

Purposeful relaxation calms the mind and muscles, controls or decreases the flow of stress hormones, reduces stress, and improves your overall well-being.

When you focus on deep breathing, you direct your body and mind towards a relaxed state. This activity promotes a healthy blood flow, releases toxins from your body, and helps in getting restorative sleep. It also promotes the flow of endorphins, which are chemicals in your brain that help you feel good while also decreasing the perception of pain.

When we experience pain, our breathing is often shallow and occurs mainly in the chest area. Our bodies perceive this as a stressful state and respond to it by increasing the heart rate or shutting down the digestive system. By practicing deep breathing, you can trigger a positive psychological response that hits reverse on the stress response. With slow and deep breathing, you can activate the parasympathetic nervous system (or the rest-and-digest system) and let your body calm down, rejuvenate and recover from the pain.

The benefits of deep breathing for pain relief are plenty. When we experience pain, our muscles tend to contract as a preventative measure along with the tightening of tissues that happens due to the tension or injury. As we breathe deeply, hormones such as nitrous oxide increase in the body and reduce the tension in the body's connective tissues and muscles, thus relieving us from pain.

Improved stress management

When we are stressed, our thoughts get automatically routed towards past regrets or future worries. All such thoughts lead to an increase in the release of stress hormones like cortisol. Thankfully, there is a free tool to manage stress effectively – your breath.

With deep, anchored breathing, you can reach a calmer and more focused state of mind. It might also help you in feeling the energy of your emotions, especially the overwhelming ones that you have been trying to escape. During stressful situations, deep breathing enables the body to release tensions instead of holding them within. This is very important, especially because storing up energy has the potential of manifesting as muscle tension or other physical illnesses.

While both parts of our nervous system are equally active, deep breathing can help in calming down the sympathetic nervous system that controls the fight-or-flight response. Due to this, the feelings of stress and anxiety take a back seat. According to Dr. Kristoffer Rhoades, a clinical neuropsychologist at UW Medicine Memory and Brain Wellness Center, "It is not possible to turn the sympathetic nervous system off completely, but I think of shifting one's breathing to a modulated, slow, relaxed pattern of not overly deep inhales and exhales as a way to turn the volume down on it." (Princing, 2021)

This practice can help deal with day-to-day anxiety problems and other persuasive disorders like generalized anxiety disorder.

Enhanced immunity

Practitioners of yoga have said it for centuries – deep, focused breathing is the key to a healthy mind and body.

In our normal or "shallow" breathing practice, we only use a part of our lung capacity for breathing. But with deep breathing, we guide air into the deepest parts of our lungs, relax tense muscles and signal our brain to lower the flow of stress hormones.

Deep breathing exercises also positively impact our immunity. With the continuous engagement of the body with deep breathing, our immunity improves in the following ways:

Lowering the blood pressure

Boosting blood flow in arteries

Decreasing the production of cortisol (stress hormone) in the body

Clearing out mucus or debris from the respiratory tract

Improving the body's autonomic response to stress

According to a study conducted in 2005 with cancer patients as subjects, it was observed that regular deep breathing exercises could help in boosting the immune cells that can combat cancer progressions. The study showed that the natural killer or NK cells (important for our body's immune system) increased with controlled, rhythmic deep breathing over a three to six month period (Kochupillai, 2005). While it may not be a quick fix, deep breathing is a step in the right direction.

Another fantastic benefit of deep breathing that improves our immunity is an efficient supply of oxygen to all parts of the body. The more you focus on breathing deeply, the more oxygen you supply to the blood in your veins. Oxygenated blood transports essential vitamins and minerals to all parts of the body, thus absorbing the nutrients effectively. The better the absorption of nutrients, the stronger your body becomes to fight off any illness.

Higher energy levels

Since deep breathing is a slow and calming exercise, many people think it lowers energy levels and causes the body to feel more tired. However, the exact opposite is true. Whether it is swimming, boxing, fighting, or even brisk walking, having control over your breath is essential. A well-controlled breathing mechanism translates into higher energy levels in the body.

Most of us are chest-breathers. It means that our breaths are very shallow, and we end up not getting as much oxygen as we could. What we need are long and deep breaths that activate our belly.

When we take a deep breath, our stomach expands outwards, and the lower ribs expand sideways. These expansions cause our diaphragm to contract. It fills our body with oxygen and slows down our respiratory rate while balancing the 'speed up' and 'speed down' mechanisms. The equilibrium calms our minds and improves focus. At the same time, these controlled breaths regulate the level of noradrenaline, a natural chemical messenger found in our bodies. The correct levels of noradrenaline influence brain activity in a way that enhances our attention.

With enhanced attention spans, the feelings of lethargy and sluggishness take a back seat, and you feel more energized to carry out your daily activities.

Effective weight management

When we talk about weight management, particularly weight loss, we instantly think about limiting the intake of calories while engaging in strenuous physical activity. While these ideas are highly effective, deep breathing helps in your weight loss journey too. According to a study conducted by experts in 2019, deep breathing exercises such as yoga can improve the metabolic activity of our brain and decrease the body mass index or BMI in teens with obesity (Upadhyah & Sharma, 2019).

Deep breathing supports our central nervous system. According to Baxter Bell, a yoga instructor and acupuncturist, "deep breathing exercises or restorative yoga may help you reduce weight by activating the parasympathetic nervous system. This part of the nervous system counteracts stress by calming your mind and balancing your body. By slowing your metabolism, it aids in digestion, which can help you lose weight. On the other hand, too much stress may cause more rapid, shallow breathing, a quicker heartbeat, and tight muscles, which may cause anxiety and less ability to quell cravings." (Shea, n.d.).

While exercising every day might not be everyone's cup of tea, deep and controlled breathing can make the desire to become fit achievable.

Deep breathing comes with a myriad of benefits and can impact our lives in more ways than one. So, it's time for you to focus on the way you breathe and provide your body with all the oxygen it needs.

Breathing Techniques for Heart and Brain Health

Breathing is not rocket science. We do it every moment. But mindful breathing requires you to keep your focus intact. Many proven techniques focus on the breath. These techniques focus on different aspects of breathing and impact your physical and mental well-being at different levels. While some techniques can be practiced on your own, a few others require guidance from a trained professional. However, you can practice them later by yourself once you have undergone training for some time.

There are many breathing exercises or techniques for you to choose from. Here are a few techniques that can help you get started:

Mindful breathing

As is evident from the name, mindful breathing requires you to concentrate on your breath and use this attention as a form of meditation. Usually, people suffering from issues such as stress, anxiety, high blood pressure or sleep issues opt for mindful breathing techniques.

There are many mindful breathing techniques. The common point in all of these techniques is your focus on the way you breathe. You need to concentrate on the natural rhythm of breathing in and out without deliberately altering the pattern. Doing this will naturally slow down the breathing pattern, making you feel calm and relaxed. It becomes a form of calming meditation as you focus on how the air moves in and out through your lungs, mouth, and nose.

Prior to practicing any meditation techniques and to get the most out of them, it is recommended that you:

Find a quiet corner that can keep you away from distractions
Choose a comfortable position (ideally sitting upright or lying down)
To perform mindful breathing techniques:
Focus on breathing by listening to the inhalation and exhalation of air through your body
Let thoughts pass without being judgmental about them.

Mantra breathing

This breathing technique requires you to chant a soothing mantra while you focus on your breath. A mantra is a phrase or word that you repeat to yourself to create focus. Some believe that meditation mantras release calming energies and vibes that soothe your mental well-being.

To perform mantra breathing:

Chant a mantra multiple times to avoid distractions
Focus on breathing as the air goes in and out of your body

Box or square breathing

This breathing technique involves creating a visualization to create focus. The technique focuses on slowing down the breathing pace and improving concentration power.

Medically, the best posture for practicing box or square breathing techniques is by sitting in a straight and upright position. By sitting up straight, it becomes easier to breathe in and breathe out fully. You can make the upper body feel more relaxed by resting your palms upward in your lap or on your knees.

To perform square or box breathing:

Sit in an upright position
Breathe in through your nose until the count of four and fill up your lungs with oxygen
Hold your breath for the count of four
Breathe out slowly through your mouth for a count of four while completely emptying your lungs
Wait for a count of four before starting the cycle again

Alternate nostril breathing

This technique is one of the most revered breathing practices in yoga. If you want to break free from the shackles of anxiety or stress, this may be the best breathing technique for you.

Most people use one nostril more than the other without even realizing it. This breathing technique can help in balancing out the breathing and eventually calming the breathing process and relieving you of stress.

The best way of practicing the alternate nostril breathing technique is by sitting in a comfortable position on the chair or lying straight on the floor. Before beginning the exercise, it is important to breathe out fully and empty the lungs.

To perform alternate nostril breathing:

Sit in an upright position on a chair or lie straight on the floor
Close your right nostril with the thumb of one hand
Breathe in through your left nostril
Close the left nostril with the fourth finger and release the thumb
Breathe out through the right nostril
Breathe in through the right nostril
Close the right nostril with the thumb and remove the fourth finger
Breathe out through the left nostril

4-7-8 breathing

Popularized by Dr. Andrew Weil, founder and Director of the Andrew Weil Center for Integrative Medicine at the University of Arizona, this breathing method is helpful for anyone experiencing a disturbed sleep cycle. This exercise can help ease the mind before going to sleep, thus ensuring that you wake up from a sound sleep.

This technique involves focusing on the breath while counting numbers. This can help distract the mind from stress and worries as you try to fall asleep. By continuing to practice this technique, your breathing might also become regular, and the body will become relaxed.

Before starting this exercise, you should practice resting the tip of your tongue against the roof of your mouth, try to relax your muscles, and breathe out from your mouth.

To perform the 4-7-8 breathing technique:

Sit in an upright position on a chair or lie straight on the floor
Breathe in through your nose for a count of four
Hold your breath for a count of seven
Part your lips and exhale loudly for a count of eight
Repeat four cycles

Diaphragmatic breathing

If you are suffering from the symptoms of lung conditions, stress, or anxiety, you should consider trying the diaphragmatic breathing technique.

Diaphragmatic breathing or belly breathing is usually a part of the pulmonary rehabilitation program. It helps in strengthening the lungs and making them work more efficiently. Pulmonary rehabilitation is an education and exercise program designed to raise your knowledge of your lungs and your disease. Lessons are held in a group format so that you can meet individuals who have the same condition as you and provide and receive peer support. By boosting your fitness level, you will grow stronger. Exercising your lungs and muscles makes you more active, allowing you to spend more time with your loved ones doing the activities you enjoy.

If the diaphragm doesn't work fully, our bodies usually rely on other muscles for breathing, usually the ones near the back, neck, or chest.

Before practicing the belly breathing technique, it is essential to relax your neck and shoulders, as this will make the diaphragm do more of the work of breathing. If you perform this technique while lying down, it may help you focus on filling the lungs fully, as you can pay close attention to the belly rising and falling.

To perform diaphragmatic breathing:

Place the hands lightly on your belly
Breathe in through your nose until your belly rises
Breathe out through your mouth for twice as long
Repeat the entire process

The Wim Hof Method

The Wim Hof Method is one of the most effective deep breathing techniques that invigorates our nervous system. The method is simple, easy, and highly effective in stimulating deep physiological processes and is backed by years of scientific study (Wim Hof Method, n.d.).

The Wim Hof Method brings many benefits to the table. It has physical and mental benefits such as increased energy, natural anti-inflammation, a boosted immune system, better sleep, quicker workout recovery, lower blood pressure, pain and mood regulation, stress control, and improved mindset.

At the time of the writing of this book, I had been practicing the Wim Hof Method of breathing every day for over 10 months In my case, it helps in the general uplifting of my mood with very little to no rumination. It has also helped improve my strength and flexibility while allowing me to hold my breath for up to four minutes. My body feels even more rejuvenated than it was in my 30s and 40s.

To perform the Wim Hof breathing technique:

Sit or lie down in a comfortable place and begin to breathe consciously

Slowly breathe from your belly so that air fills up your lungs completely

Exhale slowly without forcing it

Repeat it for 30-40 exhales

After the final exhale, hold your breath as long as possible
When you're feeling uncomfortable holding your breath, take one more deep breath and hold it for fifteen seconds
Release the breath
Repeat the cycle for three to four rounds

Wim Hof's YouTube channel offers many free guided breathing instructional videos: https://www.youtube.com/user/wimhof1

Brain Healthy Breathing Exercises for Beginners

Engaging in strenuous breathing exercises requires discipline and willpower. Think about including these techniques in your daily routine! While you have all the willpower you need, the following breathing exercises will help you develop the necessary discipline to practice complex techniques.

Start your day with morning breathing

This is a great exercise to relieve stiff muscles and clear your respiratory tract when you get up in the morning. To do this exercise, follow the following steps:

Stand up and bend forward from the waist. Keep the knees slightly bent forward. Let your arms dangle loosely to the floor.
Inhale slowly and deeply.
Roll your body up slowly, lifting your abdomen, chest, and shoulders before your head. Do not try to stand up quickly with your headfirst.

Once you are in a full standing position, hold your breath.

As you begin to bend forward again, exhale slowly. Repeat this several times to loosen your body.

Renew your energy at midday with the stimulating breathing technique

This exercise is used in yoga. It can increase your energy and help you to feel more alert. To do this exercise, follow the following steps:

Keep your mouth closed, then inhale and exhale rapidly through your nose. Keep your breaths as short as possible. Don't worry if you make a lot of noise.

Try to breathe in and out in rapid succession three times in one second. This makes the diaphragm work hard. After each set of three, breathe normally.

Be careful and do this exercise for only 15 seconds when you first begin. With practice, slowly increase the duration of the exercise by five seconds each time.

Relax at the end of the day with the 4-7-8 breathing exercise

This exercise is intended to relax and calm your body and mind. Refer to "Breathing Techniques for Heart and Brain Health" for detailed instructions.

Start your day with these breathing exercises and pump oxygen around your body and brain. You don't need any special equipment to practice these exercises. All you need is a quiet corner, and you're good to go! Now that you know these techniques, use them to reduce stress and anxiety levels while improving the health of your heart and mind.

Chapter 8
Love and Belonging

The WFPB lifestyle has been proven to improve one's quality of life. While a WFPB diet is one aspect of achieving a healthy lifestyle, another critical aspect is leading a life with love and belonging.

Humans have an innate need to socialize (or be with) other humans. Giving and receiving love and being a part of a community contributes to you being healthier and happier. When we say that our heart is 'heavy' with grief or that we have a 'broken heart', we aren't just metaphorical. In fact, medical research reveals that we can even die of a broken heart.

Love is good for your heart. It can keep stress and anxiety at bay while bringing good mental as well as cardiovascular health. In this chapter, we will explore the impact of love and belonging on the life of a human being.

Emotions and Heart Health Go Hand in Hand

Throughout the world, ancient people have appreciated the relationship between our emotions and our heart. The heart and the mind are connected very intimately. When negative states of mind such as anger, depression, anxiety, sadness or loneliness occur, the risk of heart diseases may increase. In many cases, these negative emotions also lead to the worsening of already existing heart diseases.

When someone says they have a "broken heart," they might not be saying it metaphorically. Medical science has defined this emotional situation and called it "broken heart syndrome" or cardiomyopathy. Studies have revealed that the risk of a heart attack increases nearly 21-fold within 24 hours of losing a loved one.

Our heart's health can be hampered by any stressful news. Even strong emotions such as anger can lead to irregular heart rhythms.

As we have already discussed in the previous chapters, stress can also be harmful to your heart. If you are under stress, your blood pressure and heart rate shoot up rapidly. Chronic stress exposes your body to unhealthy and persistently elevated levels of stress hormones like cortisol and may also change the way blood clots. All of these factors can set the stage for a heart attack or stroke.

Negative emotions may also affect lifestyle habits, which in turn can increase heart disease risk. For example, chronically stressed, anxious, depressed, or angry people may be more likely to drink too much alcohol, smoke, overeat, and get less exercise — all unhealthy habits that are bad for their heart.

For people who already suffer from heart disease, any form of emotional stress can further exacerbate the situation. Patients who suffer from heart diseases and anxiety are twice as likely to die within three years of a cardiac event.

Also, heart disease patients are three times as likely to be depressed. For those newly diagnosed with heart disease, depression increases the risk that a harmful heart-related event will occur within that year. Even in people with no prior heart disease, major depression doubles the risk of dying from heart-related causes.

How can we treat the situation?

If there were a 'magic pill' for curing sadness, anxiety, or depression, I would have recommended it right away. Unfortunately, no such pill has been produced so far. Medically prescribed antidepressants are available for those with severe depression. Since the heart and mind co-exist, we need to acknowledge all kinds of emotions, especially those that overwhelm our lives. Our focus should be on finding ways to take care of our emotional well-being, for which our hearts will thank us later.

The following two tips can help you keep your heart healthy:

Acknowledge your feelings: Most of the time, we run away from our feelings, especially when negative. By avoiding the feeling, we feel that we can skip the sadness and be okay with the situation. However, refusing to acknowledge sad feelings leads to bad emotional health.

Since our emotions and heart are interconnected, it also leads to disturbed cardiovascular health.

To keep your heart and mind healthy, it is essential to recognize your feelings and express them. There is no rocket science in expression. All you need to do is talk to your loved ones about how you are feeling. Find someone you can be open with and tell them the good as well as the bad.

If you are not the vocal kind, pen down your feelings in a journal. Writing is a good way of letting emotions out instead of piling them up. While writing, don't worry about the grammar, vocabulary or syntax. Just focus on expression.

After finding an outlet, if you still feel that you aren't okay, it is advisable to consult a mental health care professional. Through their guided healing treatment, the professional would help you acknowledge and overcome your feelings.

Engaging in enjoyable activities and communities

Our heart needs love and belonging. If we engage ourselves in enjoyable activities that stimulate joy and creativity along with community connection, it can help in elevating mood. Engaging in activities like healthy cooking classes, dance or art sessions, pottery classes, etc., are some of the best ways of connecting with others while nurturing your heart.

Apart from joining some fun-filled sessions, connecting with nature also helps in raising mood. It increases happiness and lowers stress levels. Go to a local trail or hike to the nearest hilltop a few times every month and notice how it takes away your stress. In doing so, you can also sign up with the local hiking community and make new friends on the way.

I walk my dog, Molly, through the local conservation area every day for at least half an hour. The forest and nature surround us, and it has a calming, stress-reducing effect on both of us. No matter the activity, stress-modifying behaviors help tilt the balance in favor of your health, decreasing the significant risk that stress and depressive illness play on heart health.

Recover From Spiritual Heart Diseases with Love and Belonging

When we talk about heart diseases, we often refer to the physical heart diseases that involve damage to the blood vessels, change in rhythm patterns of the heart, or any treatable issue with medicines and medical treatment. However, there is another side to heart diseases: *spiritual heart diseases.*

Spiritual heart diseases often stem from loneliness, depression, isolation, and alienation. Often, the defenses that we think protect us from spiritual heart diseases are the same ones that heighten them. According to Dr. Dean Ornish, MD, "Study after study has shown that people who feel lonely, depressed, and isolated are many times more likely to get sick and die prematurely – not only of heart disease but from virtually all causes – than those who have a sense of connection, love and community" (WebMD.com, 2005).

Being aware

Dr. Ornish, the founder, president, and director of the nonprofit Preventive Medicine Research Institute in Sausalito, California, and the author of *Love and Survival,* points out that today many people don't have an extended family they see regularly, or live in a neighborhood with two or three generations of neighbors. Many don't have a job that promises stability or go to a house of worship every week. "These things affect our survival to a much larger degree than people had once thought," he says.

In the book, he also mentions that "many people think of these as the things that you do after you have done all the 'important' stuff." By important stuff, he means diet and exercise. Due to this, people start regarding time spent with friends or family as a luxury. "We are touchy, feely creatures, we're creatures of community, and we ignore these things at our own peril," Ornish says (Ornish, 1998).

If you find yourself in a situation like this, you need to be aware of these feelings and acknowledge them. Talk about these issues with your physician or anyone you can confide in and make positive changes in your life.

Depression and the heart

"The general results of studies are that, for the most part, we believe depression is a risk factor for the development of heart disease," says Matthew Burg, PhD, associate clinical professor of medicine at Yale University School of Medicine and Columbia School of Medicine(WebMD.com, 2005).

According to Burg, in people who have already suffered a heart attack and undergone a clinical treatment to de-clog the blocked arteries, depression can have serious impacts. It can lead to a subsequent heart attack or even untimely death. Lack of social support or complete social isolation can increase the risk of heart complications and diseases.

Since our heart is a seeker of love and belonging, the best way of fighting depression is by being in a community of people and engaging in activities that make you feel happy. In addition to this, exercising and following a healthy diet can also help in fighting depression and keeping the heart young and healthy.

Talking about emotions

Not surprisingly, people find it easy to talk about their cholesterol or blood sugar issues with others but are very reluctant to talk about their psychological state. According to Burg, "People don't like being depressed but, in our society, there is a certain stigma about things like depression. When patients are not as forthcoming about these issues, it makes it that much harder to identify and treat."

If you talk to any person who has survived a heart attack, they are most likely to link depression with the heart attack. But if we take a closer look, the symptoms of depression usually predate the heart attack. In fact, the severity of heart attack can be decreased if people start talking about how they feel or express their overall emotional state beforehand.

According to Burg, "The depression after a heart attack, which we would call an adjustment problem or adjustment disorder, actually dissipates within a matter of weeks. If the symptoms persist, we're really talking about depression independent of heart disease. These emotions, when prolonged, are worth paying attention to, because of the potential effect they're having on the cardiovascular system."

Showing yourself compassion and kindness

All of us are flawed. You might have your own limitations and have made mistakes, but so does every other person, even if they seem to have their lives together.

When you remind yourself of such facts, it helps in treating yourself with kindness instead of disgust. Try affirming yourself in the same way to boost feelings of worthiness and positive self-regard – a stronger sense of self-worth can pave the way toward more meaningful relationships.

When you add compassion and kindness to the way you treat yourself, it keeps your mind steady and wards off depression and the linked cardiovascular diseases that often go with it.

Ways of dealing with spiritual heart diseases

Social relationships are fundamental to our thriving. The discomfort brought in by depression is a reminder to pay attention to these social relationships and further your happiness.

While there are many ways of dealing with spiritual heart diseases, some conventional ways help the best in fighting them. Let us look at these methods.

Strong personal relationships are the secret sauce

Whenever anyone deals with loneliness, the most common advice given is to socialize with people. While this is a very effective way of dealing with the issue, the key here is to socialize with the right people. Fighting that lonely feeling doesn't mean surrounding yourself with strangers. People can feel just as lonely or isolated in a group setting as they do by themselves.

The secret to feeling better is strengthening your social network of good friends, neighbors, or family members where you feel a sense of belonging. This means maintaining existing relationships or reaching out to long-lost loved ones to regain those ties. Forging new friendships is another way to improve health and reduce the risk factors of heart disease.

According to a study published in the Journal of Health and Social Behavior, our health outcomes can be positively impacted by both the quality and quantity of social relationships. As we grow older, our relationships forged over our lifetime become more important (Sage Journals, 2010).

The power of relying on strong personal relationships is also highlighted in the study published in PLoS Magazine. According to the study, people with strong social relationships are 50% more likely to live longer and healthier than those with weak ties (Holt-Lunstad,2010).

Adopt a pet

Pets, especially dogs and cats, offer so many benefits once they enter our lives. But the most significant advantage provided by them is the prevention of loneliness. They offer the highest order of love and companionship.

A pet can connect you with other people –walking a dog opens you up to a community of other dog-walkers, and a cute dog on a leash tends to be a people-magnet. Additionally, pets provide unconditional love, which can be an excellent salve for loneliness.

Volunteer

There is no better place to connect with other people than where people come together for the same shared purpose. Volunteering is the best way to connect with such people.

Volunteering for a cause you believe in can provide the same benefits as taking a class or joining a club: meeting others, being part of a group, and creating new experiences. But more than that, it can help you find more meaning in your life and move away from the sadness or loneliness you are feeling.

Practice self-care

It is essential to always remember that you are the most important person for yourself. When you feel lonely, be sure that you do whatever you can to take care of yourself.

When you practice self-care – eating good food, adequate sleep, exercising daily – you help yourself not just in the present but in the future also. Here's a bonus tip: Join a workout class such as Pilates or Zumba and start your fitness journey while driving up social interactions with people around you.

Consult a therapist

Loneliness and symptoms of depression perpetuate each other. The lonelier you are, the more depressed you feel, and vice versa.

Sometimes just "getting out there" and meeting other people isn't enough. It's possible to still feel lonely when you're around them, which could signify depression or social anxiety. If this is the case for you, it may be a good idea to seek psychotherapy to help with feelings of loneliness, especially if you also feel other symptoms of depression.

Some forms of therapy, especially cognitive-behavioral therapy (CBT), can help you change your thoughts and your actions to help you not only to experience less loneliness but to have more tools to prevent it. Whatever you do to combat loneliness, know that you are truly not alone, and there are many things you can do to feel more connected.

Science has it that loneliness is a more significant threat to society than obesity (American Psychological Association, 2017). Since it is all about feelings of isolation and depression, love and belonging can help reverse its effect. It is okay to feel lonely for a little while from time to time – we all do. But when the cycle keeps repeating itself, that is when you must alter your ways to enjoy life. Friendships and social support can help break the cycle of loneliness and bring in a flair of positivity in life.

Chapter 9
Live Long and Prosper; Longevity and Telomeres

Can you still hear your mom nagging you about eating green leafy vegetables? Or worse, do you now sound like your mom when you try to coax your friends or family members into giving green vegetables a try?

It turns out, our mothers have been right all the while! Eating vegetables and fruits makes a big difference in our life. By this, I don't just mean growing up tall or having big biceps like Popeye (or your favorite superhero!). There is scientific evidence that eating a balanced diet filled with fruits and vegetables can add years to your life.

All of us want to live long. But very few of us take the proper steps to boost our longevity. For several decades now, research has consistently found that a vegetarian diet that is mainly made up of veggies, fruit, nuts, legumes, and wholegrains, can reduce your risk of major diseases and help you live longer.

Throughout the book, we have discussed the health benefits of a whole food, plant-based diet. In this chapter, let's look at some other notable benefits that a WFPB lifestyle has in store for us.

WFPB Diet Can Increase Telomere Length

For the longest time, all of us believed that our DNA was our destiny. If the DNA reads tall, we will be tall. If it reads stout, we will be stout. However, years of research have revealed the exciting news that our lifestyle choices can impact our DNA.

In 2009, scientist Elizabeth Blackburn and her colleagues won the Nobel Prize in Medicine for unlocking the mysteries of telomeres (The Nobel Prize, n.d.), the end caps that protect our chromosomes (that are a part of our DNA). To understand it better, consider telomeres to be like the plastic tips of a shoelace. When they get damaged, the shoelaces (our chromosomes) become frayed and no longer do their job well. Telomeres are shortened every time our cells replicate and naturally shorten as we age. An unhealthy lifestyle can also shorten them – poor diet, lack of exercise and sleep, smoking, obesity, and stress or anxiety.

Over the last decade, many studies have revealed a positive association between the length of telomeres and the state of our health, especially in regard to chronic illnesses like cardiovascular diseases, diabetes, etc. The results of all these studies have shown one thing: *longer telomeres, longer life.*

The September 2013 issue of The Lancet, a medical publication, featured one of the first studies to determine the effects of lifestyle on telomere length. Researchers Dean Ornish, MD, Elizabeth Blackburn, Ph.D., and colleagues reported that a comprehensive lifestyle shift resulted in elongated telomeres in men with low-risk prostate cancer. The lifestyle changes included a low-fat, plant-based diet, moderate daily exercise, stress management, and social support. This intervention group increased telomere length by ten percent, while those in the control group had a three percent reduction in telomere length after five years.

The key idea is simple: Nutrition has a significant impact on the length of our telomeres. A plant-based diet that includes vegetables, fruits, seeds, nuts, and legumes is linked to longer telomeres and a longer lifespan.

The longest-living people throughout the world eat lots of beans, no meat, little fish, slash sugar, snack on nuts, sourdough, or 100% whole wheat bread. Fluids consumed by the longest living people: mostly water, coffee, tea, and red wine. These findings were documented in Dan Buettner's book The Blue Zones Solution: Eating and Living Like the World's Healthiest People (Buettner, 2015).

Dan Buettner clearly shows how to transform your health using smart nutrition, lifestyle, and fitness habits obtained from longevity research on the diets, eating habits, and lifestyle practices of the communities he's identified as "Blue Zones"—those places with the world's longest-lived, and thus healthiest, people, including locations such as Okinawa, Japan; Ikaria, Greece; Costa Rica's Nicoya Peninsula; Sardinia, Italy; and Loma Linda, California.

So, stop ditching those green leafy vegetables or citrus fruits for junk food items. If you want to prioritize health, it's time to follow a WFPB lifestyle.

Secrets of the longest-living people

Switch to a 90%-100% plant-based diet:

The mantra of longest living people is simple: *Your diet should be 90%-100% plant based.*

Nearly all the centenarians eat a very impressive amount of garden vegetables and leafy greens like spinach, kale, chards, and collards when they are seasonal. In the off-season, they opt for dried or pickled versions of these nutritious vegetables. Beans, greens, sweet potatoes, whole grains, fruits, nuts, and seeds dominate some meals all year long.

Say goodbye to meat

Meat is a strict no-no. Average consumption rates suggest that the Blue Zone residents consume less than two ounces of meat every month. In fact, meat is only consumed as a part of a celebratory meal or as a way to add flavor to dishes.

In place of meat, people usually prefer tofu, which is laden with protein and cancer-fighting phytoestrogens.

According to a 12-year-long study (Orlich et al., 2013) conducted on nearly 96,000 Americans living in a Blue Zone community called Loma Linda, people who lived the longest were plant-eaters or pesco-vegetarians who ate minimal amounts of fish in some form or the other. In the same region, vegetarians were more likely to outlive their non-vegetarian counterparts.

While completely cutting down meat will be difficult, start by changing the proportion of plant and animal-based foods on your plate. By doing so, you will accustom your mind to the idea of eating more WFPB food items, and your body will eventually get used to it.

You can start by adding salads and legumes to your new diet and reducing the intake of dairy products. Gradually, continue swapping the animal-based items with the WFPB ones in your favorite recipes. For instance, swap soft cheese with tofu or soy and enjoy the new dish!

Welcome beans in your diet

Beans are the ultimate kings of diets consumed by people living in Blue Zones and are the cornerstone of every longevity diet in the world: Black beans in Nicoya; lentils, garbanzo, and white beans in the Mediterranean; and soybeans in Okinawa.

Research has it that most centenarians eat at least four times as many beans as Americans (U.S. Department of Health and Human Services and U.S. Department of Agriculture, 2015) do on average — at least a half cup per day. And so should you. Why? Beans are packed with the most nutrients per gram than any other food on earth after green leafy vegetables.

On average, beans are made up of 21% protein, 77% complex carbohydrates, and only a few percent fat. Because they are fiber-rich and satisfying, they are very likely to help push less healthy foods out of your diet.

Go sour on bread

Going sour on life can be prevented if you go sour on bread. It is so because most of the breads readily available around us are made with bleached, white flour which converts into sugar on consumption and spikes insulin levels. As much as possible, strive to eat sourdough or 100% whole wheat bread.

Whole grains have higher levels of fiber than most used bleached flours. Some traditional Blue Zone breads are made by using the naturally occurring bacteria called lactobacilli, which "digests" the starches and glutens while making the bread rise.

The process also creates an acid – the "sour" in sourdough. The result is bread with less gluten with a longer shelf life and a pleasantly sour taste that most people like. Try it; you will love it!

Go whole

Consuming whole foods is one of the biggest secrets of all centenarians.

Most of the food items that they consume are made up of a single ingredient that is either raw, cooked, steamed, ground, or fermented, and not highly processed like the readily available counterparts available in the supermarket. They eat fruits, vegetables, nuts, and seeds. They grind the whole grains on their own and simmer them slowly.

They are fans of fermentation, which is an ancient way to make nutrients bioavailable. They use the process to prepare the tofu, sourdough bread, wine, and pickled vegetables they eat.

They rarely ingest artificial preservatives. Blue Zone dishes typically contain a half dozen or so ingredients, simply blended.

WFPB Has More Health Benefits Than Animal-Based Diet

That's true! A plant-based lifestyle doesn't just increase lifespan but also improves the overall quality of life.

According to a study that was published by the American College of Cardiology, "High animal protein intake was positively associated with mortality and high plant protein intake was inversely associated with mortality, especially among individuals with at least one lifestyle risk factor. Substitution of plant protein for animal protein, especially that from processed red meat, was associated with lower mortality, suggesting the importance of protein source." (Song et al., 2016)

The same study showed some striking numbers:

A meat-based diet was associated with a two percent increase in overall mortality risk and specifically an eight percent increase in risk of death from cardiovascular disease.

Conversely, a plant rich diet was associated with a ten percent reduction in overall mortality risk and a 12% reduction in cardiovascular risk.

The study revealed that the impact of animal protein on all causes of mortality was negligible, but its impact on cardiovascular death was an eye-opener. In case of a plant-based diet, all causes of mortality (including cardiovascular causes) show a dramatic decline.

The study was conducted on a group of people who already have one unhealthy lifestyle factor from the list mentioned below:

Obesity or overweight
Lack of physical activity
Significant alcohol intake
Smoking

If the impact on such individuals is so positive, imagine the effect that the WFPB lifestyle can have on people already following a good lifestyle!

WFPB Lifestyle Keeps Your Brain Healthy

While there are hundreds of physiological benefits of following a WFPB lifestyle, there are mental benefits too. A WFPB lifestyle can slow down or reverse the cognitive decline that is usually expected in old age.

According to the review of nine studies published in Frontiers in Aging Neuroscience in 2017, consuming an extra 100 grams of fruits every day could reduce the risk of cognitive decline or dementia by 13% (Jiang et al., 2017). The reason for this is simple: fruits are rich in antioxidants and polyphenols. The abundance of these plant compounds in this form of diet help in slowing down the effects of Alzheimer's disease, cognitive impairment, and dementia in old age. So start including fruits, vegetables, beans, and nuts in your diet to stay mentally fit and healthy even in your old age. A healthy mind paves the way for a healthy life!

The Whole Food, Plant-Based Lifestyle Reduces the Risk of Heart Diseases

You know that a plant-based diet is cleaner and healthier. But did you know that by going meat-free, you can reduce the risk of heart diseases by as much as 25 percent?

In general, studies suggest that people with the highest meat consumption have an increased risk of cancer, heart disease, stroke, diabetes, infections, and other conditions. By contrast, a balanced plant-based diet – high in antioxidants and fiber, low in saturated fat, with sufficient protein and essential nutrients – can reduce your risk of disease and increase longevity (remember the telomeres?).

Here's how going meat-free may protect you from the leading killers

Heart diseases and stroke

You're doing your heart a favor by eating foods acquired from plants with the least amount of processing possible. Plants include critical nutrients that are difficult to obtain from other foods and are beneficial to your heart. The minerals, vitamins, fiber, phytochemicals, and antioxidants offered by WFPB food items keep your cells healthy and your heart happy. According to expert doctors, a WFPB diet strengthens your immune system and helps fight against harmful germs and microbes.

Food items sourced from animals, directly or indirectly, come with many saturated fats. Saturated fats are known to increase the cholesterol levels in the body, thus contributing to an increase in plaquing of your arteries and making you prone to cardiac illnesses. On the other hand, WFPB food items are rich in unsaturated fatty acids (or good fat) that help keep cholesterol levels under control and cardiac disorders like heart attack and stroke at bay. In fact, a study showed that a plant based diet reduces the risk of heart diseases by as much as 25%, and going meatless can even reverse existing heart diseases (Kim et al., 2019).

Cancer

The risk of the disease can be reduced by practicing a plant-based lifestyle.

The risk of cancer has increased for everyone over time due to many factors, including pollution, the consumption of unhealthy food, and chronic stress. However, studies have revealed that a WFPB diet effectively lowers the risk of several types of cancers including gastrointestinal or colorectal cancer, and breast cancer (*Tatamango-Bartley, 2013*). Considering all types of cancer, the study revealed that the risk can be reduced by as much as 8%-10%. The fiber, antioxidants, and phytochemicals present in whole plant foods are significant contributors to a lowered cancer risk.

A meat-based diet has high levels of saturated fatty acids, which are linked to higher rates of some kinds of cancer. Red meat is linked to an increased risk of lung, pancreatic, colorectal, breast, and prostate cancer, among many others. According to a report, every three-ounce portion of red meat eaten daily increases the risk of colorectal, pancreatic and prostate cancer by as much as 17 percent (World Health Organization, 2015).

Alzheimer's Disease

Fruits, vegetables and legumes are very effective against cognitive impairment and dementia, whereas a meat-based diet (especially one rich in processed meat) is linked with an increased risk of dementia.

A plant-based diet serves as a natural source of brain-boosting vitamins. Vitamins such as B6, B12, and folic acid are key components to reducing the amount of homocysteine in the blood. This compound is associated with a higher risk of stroke and cognitive disorders such as Alzheimer's and dementia.

A recent study conducted on 30,000 people, published in Neurology, (Smyth, 2015) revealed that diets rich in healthier foods such as fruits, vegetables, and grains were linked with a reduced risk of cognitive decline commonly associated with dementia or other cognitive disorders. Diets higher in these healthier foods showed a reduced risk of up to 24%, while diets higher in saturated fat and red meat showed higher risks.

There are many theories that attempt to explain the memory-boosting properties of plant-based diets. One such theory behind the brain boost from plant-based eating is that a diet rich in fruits and veggies, particularly those that are dark green, leafy, or brightly colored, is richer in antioxidants than a typical omnivore diet. These antioxidants are constantly on patrol in the body and not only fight inflammation that can lead to injury of the brain tissues, but also identify and remove free radicals (unstable atoms that can damage cells) before they can cause problems. This means that your favorite smoothie is a delicious way to consume more antioxidant-rich foods on a daily basis.

Type II diabetes

One of the most significant benefits of switching to a plant-based diet is that it reduces the risk of type II diabetes. The reason is simple: A plant-based lifestyle helps in keeping your weight and basal metabolic rate (BMR) under check. When you cannot control your weight, the accumulated fatty acid cushions the cells and makes them resistant to insulin. But with a plant-based diet, you are less likely to be obese and, in turn, diabetic.

In the case of type II diabetes, our diet can significantly impact our well-being. Research conducted in 2016 revealed that eating a diet rich in whole plant foods rich in fiber reduces the risk of developing type II diabetes by nearly 34% (National Institutes of Health, 2013). This is so because a WFPB diet is free of saturated fats that increase cholesterol levels in the body. With lower levels of cholesterol, chances of developing type II diabetes are greatly reduced. On the contrary, people who consume animal-based products, especially meat, are more prone to having a higher BMI and hence a greater risk of diabetes.

A plant-based diet also improves insulin sensitivity and glycemic control, along with weight management. This further lowers the risk of diabetes among followers of a whole food, plant-based lifestyle.

Switching to a WFPB diet is not as difficult as it seems. Start with making small changes in your diet, and you will start enjoying this routine. You will get accustomed to this lifestyle, and the health benefits that it will bring will amaze you. So get ready to welcome a happy heart and healthy life!

Conclusion

I have consumed my fair share of junk and processed foods over the years in the name of treats. But here's the catch: It was never a treat. In fact, it was the exact opposite of what a treat is! The human body is one of the most complex machines on this planet, yet we abuse this machinery the most in the name of taste, habit, culture, lifestyle, and convenience.

There is a lot of resistance to change in the world we live in. But as more and more people like you wake up and notice the impact of our poor decisions on the poor animals and the overall planet, the better our future decisions will be. The starting point of this journey is simple: *You need to have love and compassion for yourself.* You need to respect the amazing and the only machinery that you are gifted with – and don't wait to get sick before making the lifestyle change that your body needs.

The human body is designed to survive, and survival depends on the food we eat. Physiologically, humans were created for eating plants. We are all the same species, and a wealth of studies and other evidence shows that plant-based diets can prevent, treat, and reverse almost all major chronic diseases and health conditions. Plant-based foods promote optimal energy levels, skin, hair, and nail health, healthy weight maintenance without restriction, healthy bones, hormonal balance, the list goes on!

Across various chapters covered in this book, I have laid great emphasis on these five superfoods – fruits, vegetables, legumes, whole grains, and tubers or root vegetables – and the health benefits that they bring with them. For instance, green, leafy vegetables are loaded with nutrition and have very few calories. Stalk vegetables, such as celery and asparagus, are a rich source of minerals and folic acid.

A WFPB lifestyle is not just about food. It involves many other things such as meditation, exercise, and engagement with friends and family. The benefits of doing so are simple: it reduces your risk of cardiovascular diseases and other severe ailments like cancer and Alzheimer's disease. In addition to this, it also helps bring you closer to nature and your loved ones.

When WFPB food items come with such incredible and miraculous benefits, why should we not fully embrace their power while appreciating the flavors they add to the diet? Through this book, I have tried to provide you with the diet's benefits and motivate you to try this lifestyle for yourself.

Could you eat a plant-based diet one day a week? If the answer is "yes" or even a "maybe," then start there. Start wherever you can. The most important thing is that you start. Now is the perfect time to affect change in your life, to begin a journey of love, compassion, consciousness, health, and growth. I know the thought of changing habits you have had your entire lifetime can seem daunting, but the results will be so worth it. Let's do this!

This book is a comprehensive active-living guide and mentor for current and aspiring plant-based lifestyle followers. I hope the book motivates and inspires you to increase the quality (and length!) of your life by enjoying a WFPB diet and engaging in regular meditation and exercise. If you're already enjoying a plant-based, active lifestyle, this book will support you in continuing to reach your health and fitness goals. With information about different food items, breathing and meditation techniques, some nutrient-rich recipes, at-home workouts, and lifestyle tips, you're sure to add something new to your healthy-living repertoire. If you're new to this form of lifestyle, this book will get you started on the right foot.

If you're just starting with eating a healthy, plant-based diet and becoming more active with regular exercise, you might find it to be hard work at first. But as I have mentioned throughout the book, the longer you stick with it, the easier it becomes. Healthy living doesn't have to be difficult, overwhelming, or stressful. This book assumes that, like most people, you're very busy and have many commitments in your daily life. That's why I tried to impart plenty of healthy-living tips meant to simplify your life. The goal is to provide you with the correct information about this lifestyle while also recommending some activities and recipes that you can enjoy.

Beyond diet and exercise, the book also focuses on effective breathing. Breathing affects our respiratory, neurological, cardiovascular, muscular, gastrointestinal, and psychological well-being. Recall the advice by Mladen Globulic – "You can influence asthma; you can influence chronic obstructive pulmonary disease; you can influence heart failure. There are studies that show that people who practice breathing exercises and have those conditions – they benefit."

Another thing that the book laid great emphasis on was the power of meditation in keeping evils like stress and anxiety away. Meditation can bring positive changes in your overall well-being. It can bring a sense of calm and peace that will always keep your energies high and reduce stress levels. These benefits aren't just experienced while you meditate; their positive benefits continue to make you feel better throughout the day.

If you understand and religiously follow a WFPB lifestyle, it will restore balance in your life. Prepare to train, eat and adopt a lifestyle based on achieving total fitness, health, and well-being, for a fitter, faster, stronger you! Once you've made a conscious choice to give your body the nutrition it needs to perform at an optimum level and remain in good health perpetually, the beautiful journey begins. Let this book be a guide as you take these positive steps towards total fitness.

Having practiced a whole food, plant-based lifestyle and enjoyed the plethora of health and lifestyle benefits it offers, I am very excited to see you making a conscious effort to follow the same. As you progress further in this lifestyle form, you will understand its benefits and become a fitter (physical and mental) version of yourself. You'll be choosing a lifestyle that causes the least harm possible – to your health, to the environment, and to animals. That choice will be greatly rewarded.

While I have laid down hundreds of pieces of advice across various chapters in the book, I have one final piece of advice to give you: *Don't delay your wellness journey!* Too often, I come across people who either change their lifestyle at a very late stage in life or quit before they see the positive impacts, and they lose all the progress they had made otherwise. Don't be that person. Once you have chosen to follow this lifestyle, commit to it and give it your best. It is only a matter of time until you start enjoying it and reaping the multitude of health benefits the WFPB lifestyle has to offer.

Following my advice will be easier if you define the "why" aspect of switching to this lifestyle. We're not going to stick to a healthy lifestyle just because someone told us to or because we have a vague idea that exercise and good nutrition will make us healthier. We need our very own personal, *detailed reasons*. So, start by defining your personal "why"!

In the words of one of my favorite fitness role models, Miryah Scott, "Treating your body right through proper eating and working out is about giving back to you, making time for you, conquering challenges, increasing your energy, boosting your self-confidence and, most of all, it's about feeling good."

As a bonus, caring about your health is fun! You get to try all sorts of new and delicious foods, try some new activities, and best of all, witness remarkable changes in how you look, how you feel, and how long you live (although you won't see that one until you're ninety).

Whether you are new to this lifestyle, already familiar with it, or an active follower, this book will serve as an invaluable resource and guide.

Enjoy the journey!

Appreciation Message:

Thanks for reading, and if you enjoyed the book, please consider leaving an honest review on Amazon so that I can continue to write books that help people restore their health!

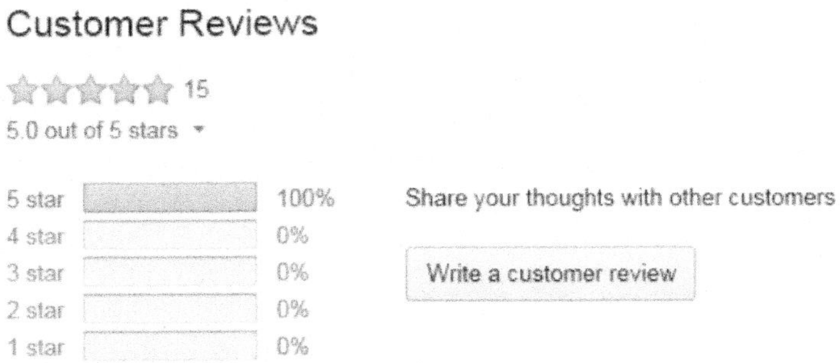

Scan the QR code below to leave a quick review:

Just For You!

A Free Gift to Our Readers

Whole Food Plant-Based Lifestyle Guide to Restore Your Health

Scan the QR code below to download:

http://bit.ly/WFPBLGuide

References

American Heart Association. (2020, November 11). *The Skinny on Fats*. Www.Heart.Org. https://www.heart.org/en/health-topics/cholesterol/prevention-and-treatment-of-high-cholesterol-hyperlipidemia/the-skinny-on-fats

American Psychological Association. (2017, September 5). *Social isolation, loneliness could be a greater threat to public health than obesity*. ScienceDaily. Retrieved January 5, 2022, from https://www.sciencedaily.com/releases/2017/08/170805165319.htm

Arts, J., Fernandez, M. L., & Lofgren, I. E. (2014, January 6). Coronary Heart Disease Risk Factors in College Students. National Center for Biotechnology Information. https://www.ncbi.nlm.nih.gov/pmc/articles/PMC3951799/

Aschwanden, C., & Aschwanden, C. (2015, August 24). *Are you risking cancer when you put that meat on the grill?* Washington Post. https://www.washingtonpost.com/national/health-science/are-you-risking-cancer-when-you-put-that-meat-on-the-grill/2015/08/24/16b41b24-45b0-11e5-8e7d-9c033e6745d8_story.html

Brinke, L., & Bolandzadeh, N. (2014, April 7). *Aerobic Exercise Increases Hippocampal Volume in Older Women with Probable Mild Cognitive Impairment: A 6-Month Randomized Controlled Trial.*

National Institutes of Health.
https://www.ncbi.nlm.nih.gov/pmc/articles/PMC4508129/

British Heart Foundation. (n.d.). *Are multivitamins good for you?* Retrieved December 27, 2021, from https://www.bhf.org.uk/informationsupport/heart-matters-magazine/news/behind-the-headlines/multivitamins

Buettner, D. (2015). *The Blue Zones Solution: Eating and Living Like the World's Healthiest People*. National Geographic.

Cardiovascular diseases. (2019, June 11). World Health Organization. https://www.who.int/health-topics/cardiovascular-diseases#tab=tab_1

Centers for Disease Control and Prevention. (2021, September 27). *Heart Disease Facts | cdc.gov*. https://www.cdc.gov/heartdisease/facts.htm

Crouch, B. M. (2019, January 8). *To Live Longer, Exercise Daily*. AARP. https://www.aarp.org/health/healthy-living/info-2019/exercise-longevity-wellness-benefits.html

Cuda, G. (2010, December 6). *Just Breathe: Body Has A Built-In Stress Reliever*. NPR.Org. https://choice.npr.org/index.html?origin=https://www.npr.org/2010/12/06/131734718/just-breathe-body-has-a-built-in-stress-reliever

Esselstyn, C. B. (2001, October 1). *Resolving the Coronary Artery Disease Epidemic Through Plant-Based Nutrition*. Wiley Online Library. https://onlinelibrary.wiley.com/doi/full/10.1111/j.1520-037X.2001.00538.x

Esselstyn, C. G. J., Gendy, G., Doyle, J., Golubic, M., & Roizen, M. F. (2014, July). A Way to Reverse CAD? DrEsselstyn.Com. https://dresselstyn.com/JFP_06307_Article1.pdf

Esselstyn, Jr, C. B. (2007, August 31). *We Can Prevent and Even Reverse Coronary Artery Heart Disease*. The National Center for Biotechnology Information. https://www.ncbi.nlm.nih.gov/pmc/articles/PMC2100124/

Fan, L., Blumenthal, J. A., Watkins, L. L., & Sherwood, A. (2015, January 14). *Work and home stress: associations with anxiety and depression symptoms*. OUP Academic. https://academic.oup.com/occmed/article/65/2/110/1488809

Faclm, G. M. M. D. (2019, October 29). The Amount of Vitamin D Supplementation I Recommend. NutritionFacts.Org. https://nutritionfacts.org/2019/04/23/the-amount-of-vitamin-d-supplementation-i-recommend/

Forks Over Knives. (2015, October 27). *What is a Whole-Food, Plant-Based Diet? [INFOGRAPHIC]*. https://www.forksoverknives.com/wellness/what-is-a-whole-food-plant-based-diet/

Fox, N. (2019). *The Many Health Risks of Processed Foods*. Laborers' Health & Safety Fund of North America. https://www.lhsfna.org/the-many-health-risks-of-processed-foods/

Gavin, J. (2021, January). *6 Health Benefits of Antioxidants*. Jessica Gavin Culinary Scientist. https://www.jessicagavin.com/benefits-of-antioxidants/

Gender differences in cardiovascular disease. (2019, December 1). ScienceDirect. https://www.sciencedirect.com/science/article/pii/S2590093519300256

Gill, J. M. R. (2012, November 21). *Physical Activity and Prevention of Type 2 Diabetes Mellitus*. SpringerLink. https://link.springer.com/article/10.2165/00007256-200838100-00002?error=cookies_not_supported&code=fb31d697-2d12-4acf-b349-c997574f4461

Harvard Health. (2019, May 1). *More evidence that exercise can boost mood*. https://www.health.harvard.edu/mind-and-mood/more-evidence-that-exercise-can-boost-mood

Heart Disease Facts | cdc.gov. (2021, September 27). Centers for Disease Control and Prevention. https://www.cdc.gov/heartdisease/facts.htm

Holt-Lunstad, J. (2010, July 27). *Social Relationships and Mortality Risk: A Meta-analytic Review*. PLOS Medicine.

https://journals.plos.org/plosmedicine/article?id=10.1371/journal.pmed.1000316#top

Jiang, X., Huang, J., Song, D., Deng, R., Wei, J., & Zhang, Z. (2017a). *Increased Consumption of Fruit and Vegetables Is Related to a Reduced Risk of Cognitive Impairment and Dementia: Meta-Analysis*. Frontiers. https://www.frontiersin.org/articles/10.3389/fnagi.2017.00018/full

Jiang, X., Huang, J., Song, D., Deng, R., Wei, J., & Zhang, Z. (2017b). *Increased Consumption of Fruit and Vegetables Is Related to a Reduced Risk of Cognitive Impairment and Dementia: Meta-Analysis*. Frontiers. https://www.frontiersin.org/articles/10.3389/fnagi.2017.00018/full

Kim, H., Caulfield, L. E., Garcia-Larsen, V., Steffen, L. M., Coresh, J., & Rebholz, C. M. (2019, September 7). *Plant-Based Diets Are Associated With a Lower Risk of Incident Cardiovascular Disease, Cardiovascular Disease Mortality, and All-Cause Mortality in a General Population of Middle-Aged Adults*. Journal of the American Heart Association. https://www.ahajournals.org/doi/10.1161/JAHA.119.012865

Kochupillai, V. (2005, November). *Effect of rhythmic breathing (Sudarshan Kriya and Pranayam) on immune functions and tobacco addiction*. Pubmed.Gov. Retrieved December 31, 2021, from https://pubmed.ncbi.nlm.nih.gov/16387692/

Lawler, M., & Kennedy, K. R. (2020, January 17). *9 Scientific Benefits of Following a Plant-Based Diet*. EverydayHealth.Com. https://www.everydayhealth.com/diet-nutrition/scientific-benefits-following-plant-based-diet/

Lippi, G., Mattiuzzi, C., & Cervellin, G. (2016, January 1). Meat consumption and cancer risk: a critical review of published meta-analyses. ScienceDirect. https://www.sciencedirect.com/science/article/abs/pii/S1040842815300780

Mandsager, K., MD. (2018, October 19). *Association of Cardiorespiratory Fitness With Long-term Mortality Among Adults Undergoing Exercise Treadmill*. JAMA Network. https://jamanetwork.com/journals/jamanetworkopen/fullarticle/2707428

Myers, J. (2003, January 7). *Exercise and Cardiovascular Health*. AHA Journals. https://www.ahajournals.org/doi/full/10.1161/01.cir.0000048890.59383.8d

National Institutes of Health. (2013). *Nutritional Update for Physicians: Plant-Based Diets*. PubMed Central. https://www.ncbi.nlm.nih.gov/pmc/articles/PMC3662288/

National Institutes of Health. (2014, September 16). *Association between Anger and Mental Stress-Induced Myocardial Ischemia*. https://www.ncbi.nlm.nih.gov/pmc/articles/PMC4268485/

Orlich, M. J., Singh, P. N., Sabate, J., Jaceldo-Siegl, K., Fan, J., Knutsen, S., Beeson, W. L., & Fraser, G. E. (2013, July 8). *Vegetarian Dietary Patterns and Mortality in Adventist Health Study 2*. National Institutes of Health. https://www.ncbi.nlm.nih.gov/pmc/articles/PMC4191896/

Ornish, D. (1998). *Love & Survival: The Scientific Basis for the Healing Power of Intimacy* (1st ed.). Harper.

Ornish, D. (2008, June 17). *Changes in prostate gene expression in men undergoing an intensive nutrition and lifestyle intervention*. PNAS. https://www.pnas.org/content/105/24/8369

Palikuca, S. (2019, July 12). *5 myths of whole-food plant-based diets debunked.* Find a DO | Doctors of Osteopathic Medicine. https://findado.osteopathic.org/5-myths-of-whole-food-plant-based-diets-debunked

Pathak, E. (2016, October 4). *Is Heart Disease or Cancer the Leading Cause of Death in United States Women?* National Library of Medicine, National Center for Biotechnology Information. Retrieved December 17, 2021, from https://pubmed.ncbi.nlm.nih.gov/27717539/

Princing, M. (2021, September 1). *This Is Why Deep Breathing Makes You Feel so Chill.* Right as Rain by UW Medicine. https://rightasrain.uwmedicine.org/mind/stress/why-deep-breathing-makes-you-feel-so-chill

Physicians Committee for Responsible Medicine. (2020, December 9). Nutritional Requirements throughout the Life Cycle | Nutrition Guide for Clinicians. https://nutritionguide.pcrm.org/nutritionguide/view/Nutrition_Guide_for_Clinicians/1342043/all/Nutritional_Requirements_throughout_the_Life_Cycle

Sage Journals. (2006, December 1). *Turning Up the Heat: Inflammation as a Mechanism Linking Chronic Stress, Depression, and Heart Disease*. https://journals.sagepub.com/doi/abs/10.1111/j.1467-8721.2006.00450.x

Sage Journals. (2010, October 8). *Social Relationships and Health: A Flashpoint for Health Policy*. https://journals.sagepub.com/doi/abs/10.1177/0022146510383501

Santarelli, R. L., Pierre, F., & Corpet, D. E. (2008, March 25). Processed Meat and Colorectal Cancer: A Review of Epidemiologic and Experimental Evidence. Taylor & Francis. https://www.tandfonline.com/doi/abs/10.1080/01635580701684872

Shea, L. (n.d.). *How Does Deep Breathing Help You Lose Weight? | Livestrong.com*. LIVESTRONG.COM. Retrieved December 31, 2021, from https://www.livestrong.com/article/272070-how-does-deep-breathing-help-you-lose-weight/

Smyth, A. (2015, June 2). *Healthy eating and reduced risk of cognitive decline*. Neurology. https://n.neurology.org/content/84/22/2258

Song, M., Fung, T. T., & Hu, F. B. (2016, August 2). *Association of Animal and Plant Protein Intake With Mortality*. American College of Cardiology. https://www.acc.org/latest-in-cardiology/journal-scans/2016/08/02/11/53/association-of-animal-and-plant-protein-intake

Swap Saturated Fats with Unsaturated Fats for a Healthy Heart. (2017, July 30). CardioSmart. https://www.cardiosmart.org/news/2017/7/swap-saturated-fats-with-unsaturated-fats-for-a-healthy-heart#:%7E:text=Replacing%20saturated%20fats%20with%20unsaturated,from%20the%20American%20Heart%20Association

Tantamango-Bartley, Y. (2013, February 1). *Vegetarian Diets and the Incidence of Cancer in a Low-risk Population*. Cancer Epidemiology, Biomarkers & Prevention. https://cebp.aacrjournals.org/content/22/2/286.long

The Nobel Prize. (n.d.). *Elizabeth H. Blackburn Prize presentation*. NobelPrize.Org. Retrieved January 6, 2022, from https://www.nobelprize.org/prizes/medicine/2009/blackburn/prize-presentation/

Upadhyah, A., & Sharma, D. (2019, June). *Effect of short term yoga on body weight, BMI, body fat percentage & blood pressure*.

ResearchGate.Net. Retrieved December 31, 2021, from https://www.researchgate.net/publication/333848406_Effect_of_short_term_yoga_on_body_weight_BMI_body_fat_percentage_blood_pressure

U.S. Department of Health and Human Services and U.S. Department of Agriculture. (2015, December). *2015-2020 Dietary Guidelines | health.gov*. Health.Gov. https://health.gov/our-work/nutrition-physical-activity/dietary-guidelines/previous-dietary-guidelines/2015

Valvano, L. (2018, May 31). *Deep breathing helps Anxiety and Depression*. The Stress Management Society. https://www.stress.org.uk/deep-breathing-helps-anxiety-depression/

Villines, Z. (2019, June 25). *What to know about sugar in fruit*. Medical News Today. https://www.medicalnewstoday.com/articles/325550

Wallace, R. K., & Benson, H. (1972, February). *The Physiology of Meditation. N on JSTOR*. JSTOR.Org. https://www.jstor.org/stable/24927272

Webb, D. (2013, September). *Phytochemicals' Role in Good Health*. Today's Dietitian. https://www.todaysdietitian.com/newarchives/090313p70.shtml

WebMD.com. (2005, June 1). *Many Emotions Can Damage the Heart*. WebMD.

https://www.webmd.com/depression/features/many-emotions-can-damage-heart

Wim Hof Method. (n.d.). *The Science behind the*. Retrieved December 31, 2021, from https://www.wimhofmethod.com/science

World Health Organization. (2015, October 25). *Cancer: Carcinogenicity of the consumption of red meat and processed meat*. https://www.who.int/news-room/questions-and-answers/item/cancer-carcinogenicity-of-the-consumption-of-red-meat-and-processed-meat#:%7E:text=However%2C%20if%20the%20association%20of,of%20red%20meat%20eaten%20daily.

World Health Organization. (2021, June 11). *Cardiovascular diseases (CVDs)*. https://www.who.int/news-room/fact-sheets/detail/cardiovascular-diseases-(cvds)

Printed in Great Britain
by Amazon

22226546R00098